"PAM'S WRITING SPEAKS TO THE PLACE WHERE PEOPLE ARE living. With sensitivity and insight, Pam gently prompts the reader to take a new direction. She brings hope and healing where before there was only darkness. I'd recommend this book to be read again and again."

H. NORMAN WRIGHT, COUNSELOR AND AUTHOR OF
*RECOVERING FROM THE LOSSES OF LIFE* AND
*WHY DID THIS HAPPEN TO ME?*

"IN PAM VREDEVELT'S GENTLE YET KNOWLEDGEABLE STYLE, we are taken by the hand and shown how to hang onto hope while letting go of disappointments and recovering joy from painful losses. Whether it is you who has suffered a loss, or someone you dearly love, you will be thankful you found this book."

LISA WHELCHEL, AUTHOR OF
*THE FACTS OF LIFE AND*
*OTHER LESSONS MY FATHER TAUGHT ME*

# Letting Go

## OF
## DISAPPOINTMENTS
## AND
## PAINFUL LOSSES

## PAM VREDEVELT

Multnomah® Publishers *Sisters, Oregon*

LETTING GO OF DISAPPOINTMENTS AND PAINFUL LOSSES
published by Multnomah Publishers, Inc.

© 2001 by Pam Vredevelt
International Standard Book Number: 1-57673-954-6

Cover design by The Office of Bill Chiaravelle
Cover image by Artville

Unless otherwise noted, Scripture quotations are from *The Holy Bible,*
New International Version © 1973, 1984 by International Bible Society,
used by permission of Zondervan Publishing House.

Also quoted:
*The Amplified Bible* (AMP) © 1965, 1987 by Zondervan Publishing House.
*The Message* © 1993 by Eugene H. Peterson.
*The Living Bible* (TLB) ©1971. Used by permission of
Tyndale House Publishers, Inc. All rights reserved.
*New American Standard Bible* (NASB) © 1960, 1977, 1995
by the Lockman Foundation. Used by permission.
*The Holy Bible,* New King James Version (NKJV) © 1984 by Thomas Nelson, Inc.

*Multnomah* is a trademark of Multnomah Publishers, Inc.,
and is registered in the U.S. Patent and Trademark Office.
The colophon is a trademark of Multnomah Publishers, Inc.

For information:
MULTNOMAH PUBLISHERS, INC. • P.O. BOX 1720 • SISTERS, OR 97759

Library of Congress Cataloging-in-Publication Data

Vredevelt, Pam W., 1955–
    Letting go of disappointments and painful losses / by Pam Vredevelt.
        p. cm.
Includes bibliographical references.
ISNBN 1-57673-954-6 (pbk.)
1. Consolation. 2. Disappointment—Religious aspects, Christianity.
3. Loss (Psychology)—Religious aspects—Christianity. I. Title.
BV4909.V74 2001
248.8'6—dc21                                          2001003318

01 02 03 04 05—10 9 8 7 6 5 4 3 2 1 0

To my father,
Charles S. Walker,
who has skillfully let go of significant
disappointments and painful losses in his life.
Thank you for faithfully hanging on to God and
wisely investing the gifts and talents God has given you.
I want to follow in your footsteps.

# CONTENTS

# ACKNOWLEDGMENTS

BILL JENSEN, YOU ARE A VISIONARY WITH A SIXTH SENSE about the publishing world. Thank you for inviting me to do the Letting Go series. I continue to be a bit baffled by your confidence in me. But it keeps me humbly on my knees, asking God to show me what He wants to say through this less-than-perfect vessel.

Holly Halverson, you have bolstered me in the editing process with your encouraging feedback and sharp mind on task. Thank you for your excellent questions, which have caused me to clarify my message and carefully consider my word choice. It is a delight to team with you.

Judith St. Pierre, I appreciate your structural precision and ability to skim the dross off of my manuscript. You know how to bring the gold to the surface and make a writer look good.

I'd also like to say a special thanks to David Webb for adding your refining touches to this book at a time when you were buried with many other projects. I appreciate the sacrifices you made on my behalf.

Don and Brenda Jacobson, I see God's hand on you, and it is a great privilege to partner with you for the kingdom. You facilitate the penetration of God's light into darkness. Thank you for counting the cost, paying the price, and persevering. I believe that what God has ahead for you is absolutely going to blow your mind.

John, Jessie, Ben, and Nathan, you have taught me many lessons about holding things loosely and letting go. Thank you for your love and support as I've pecked away at the keyboard through the years. Your enthusiasm for my books puts a smile on my face.

# INTRODUCTION

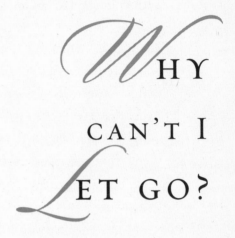

# Why can't I Let Go?

IN MY COUNSELING OFFICE AND DURING MY TRAVELS AS A speaker, I frequently hear these kinds of questions from men and women:

"How can I let go of my disappointment?"

"How do I move on after the death of my dream?"

"How will I ever experience joy after the loss I've suffered?"

"How can I let go of the life I thought was mine and receive the best God has to give?"

These souls genuinely long for rock-solid answers in the midst of the disappointing and harsh realities of their lives.

During the last several years, I've asked more than one thousand people this question: What are you finding difficult to let go of at this time in your life? Here's what many of them said:

I am finding it hard to let go of...

10

...a friendship that went sour.

...a job I loved and lost to corporate change.

...my teenager who has gone astray.

...my shameful past.

...my spouse of fifty-two years.

...my reputation after I made a terrible mistake.

...my childhood dreams, which aren't realistic anymore.

...my son/daughter who recently married and moved away.

...my stillborn baby.

...my keepsakes that were lost in a fire.

...my expectations that things would turn out the way I wanted.

...my health.

In every season of life, we are faced with disappointing situations and disturbing emotions that we must learn to let go of for our own good. Letting go, however, requires us to confront many of the core values of our culture.

People today value competence, achievement, gain, accumulation, control, self-sufficiency, and independence. Capitalizing on our fear of losing these things, advertisers cultivate our appetites not only to hang on tight to whatever we have, but also to seek ever more "stuff" in order to feel satisfied. Television commercials hammer the message into our psyches: "The more you have, the more valued, powerful, sexy, and successful you will be." Of course, the flip side of this message is: "The less you have, the less valued, powerful, sexy, and successful you will be." It's a deceptive, toxic thesis that sets us up for disappointment and undermines our sense of contentment. Although our culture conditions us to hang on, peace and true satisfaction come with letting go.

Cheryl, a woman who came to me for counseling, told me that before she had quadruple-bypass heart surgery, she experienced a pervasive feeling of emptiness. "I bought bigger houses and nicer cars, filled more closets with clothes, and redecorated every year. I wanted more, more, more to fill the hole inside. I kept thinking, *If I just have more, the emptiness will go away.*

But Cheryl's heart attack and subsequent surgery changed things. Life-threatening situations typically do. In preparation for her hospital stay, she packed a small, dark green suitcase with a few personal belongings. All the items fit neatly in her compact canvas bag-on-wheels. During her recovery, she used the same robe, the same slippers, the same comb, and the same brush every day. She read from one of the two books she had brought with her, selected from her library of hundreds.

One afternoon, Cheryl was surprised by the contentment she felt. "I was rummaging through my suitcase, which contained five or six items from home," she said, "and it dawned on me that the emptiness was gone. The surgery had gone well.

The prognosis was good. God had granted me life. I had everything I needed." A month later, Cheryl and a friend held a three-day garage sale at which she sold much of what she had accumulated over the years. "More isn't necessarily better," she concluded. "When I let go of all that stuff, I let go of the illusions that came with it."

Cheryl's physical illness had facilitated emotional healing. The heart surgery had been successful on two counts: It had given her another chance to live, and it had helped her release her grip on the clutter that was holding her hostage.

---

*Our whole being by its very nature is one vast need;*

*incomplete, preparatory, empty yet cluttered,*

*crying out for Him who can untie things*

*that are now knotted together and*

*tie up things that are still dangling loose.*

C. S. LEWIS

---

We all have holes in our souls. But acknowledging this takes courage because we don't easily accept and embrace weakness, need, loss, or suffering. For the most part, we harbor a subtle contempt for the debilities or deficiencies we perceive in ourselves and others. As a result, we end up rejecting key parts of our humanity. We gloss over our needs rather than admit them. We deny, minimize, or at least sidestep many forms of suffering. The result? We are left to struggle with our afflictions alone in the dark.

God never intended for us to suffer alone. From the very beginning of time, He has wanted people to enjoy intimate relationships with Him and others. He longs to walk arm-in-arm with us—and to provide empathetic friends to walk with us—through the sorrows and sufferings that are an inevitable part of life in this world. Connections matter. When we withdraw, detach, or close God and others out of our suffering, we turn away from our source of life and derail our own healing. In relationship with God and others, however, we can find the safety to let go and begin to heal.

When I think back over my own life—the disappointments, the losses, the times of deep sadness and overwhelming anxiety—I can see that my greatest moments of relief came when I sensed that God or a trusted friend was truly present with me in my pain. It was as if someone opened the door on my darkness, walked in, sat down with me, and, with full acceptance, waited. My brokenness was our meeting place. Inner peace and healing were born within that connection. That companionship in my suffering brought relief, even though the circumstances evoking the pain remained the same.

We are all vulnerable to disappointment and painful loss. As you read the pages that follow, you will meet many people who, like you, have suffered deep sorrow. I pulled some of the stories from my personal journals. Others came from people with whom I've had the privilege of crossing paths, people who have taught me about holding things loosely. I hope the ideas and stories in this book will raise your awareness that you are not alone in your struggles and that you do not have to bear your burdens in isolation.

There is a Companion awaiting your invitation. God sees. He cares. Your painful disappointments matter to Him, and He has not abandoned you in your pain. Nor is your pain an obstacle to His work in you. Your point of brokenness may very well become the place where He moves powerfully in a holy visitation. Through various sufferings I have learned that the empty places created by letting go become the places God can fill with His richest blessings.

May God enable us all to become skilled artisans in letting go.

---

*God is a specialist when the anguish is deep.*
*His ability to heal the soul is profound...those who*
*rely on His wounded Son will find relief.*
CHUCK SWINDOLL

---

# CHAPTER ONE

# RELAX
# AND
# RECEIVE

TRY A LITTLE EXERCISE WITH ME. I'D LIKE YOU TO CLENCH your fist into a ball, squeeze as hard as you possibly can, and count to ten. Study your hand as you do so.

Ready? Go. S-q-u-e-e-e-e-z-e.

Okay, now relax. How did your fist feel, gripping so tightly? What did it look like? Can you describe the sensations you felt? How did it feel to release your grip and open your hand after you counted to ten?

When your hand was clenched, it was uncomfortable, wasn't it? Tense. Bloodless. Unable to move freely. Not only that, but it wasn't able to do what it was *designed* to do. Your hand was closed, unable to receive. But when you let go and opened your hand, you could feel the blood returning to your fingers, couldn't you? Your hand became warm again. It relaxed, the discomfort left, and you felt relief. Your fingers moved naturally, and your hand was in a much better position to receive.

There are similarities between our physical bodies and our psyches. When we go through life grasping, clinging, clutching, and desperately trying to hang on to things that should naturally be released, we ache. We get tied up in knots. We become emotionally constricted and locked up in pain. We lose freedom of movement in our lives and feel paralyzed.

None of us enjoys loss. The world teaches us to avoid it at all costs. We don't like to let go of something we treasure, love, value, or simply own. When we are forced to let go of something, it usually ends up with claw marks all over it.

Billy Graham tells a story about a small boy caught playing with an extremely valuable vase. The little guy had put his hand into the vase but couldn't take it out. His father tried his best to help him, but all his efforts were in vain.

They were thinking gloomily of breaking the beautiful vase when the father sighed and said, "Now, son, try one more time. Open your hand and hold your fingers out straight as you see me doing, and then *pull*."

To his dad's astonishment the little fellow said, "Oh no, Father. I couldn't put my fingers out like that. If I did, I'd drop my penny!"[1]

Smile if you will, but truth be told, you and I are a lot like that little boy—so busy holding on to what we should be letting go of that we cannot accept freedom.

When Carl came to see me, his wife had just told him that she had found a lover and no longer wanted to be married. Looking at the floor and shaking his head in utter disbelief, he said, "I know I have my faults, but divorce? I just never thought it would come to this." As far as his wife was concerned, the relationship was over, and Carl wanted help in adjusting to the many losses that accompanied the divorce. At sixty-four, he thought that starting over was an impossible task.

During the months that followed, Carl and Nancy divided their assets, signed papers, and committed to parting amicably. Carl moved out, purchased another home, and tried to begin a new life. After the divorce was finalized, he dated off and on but continued to call Nancy on a regular basis. Whenever he came into my office after seeing her, Carl was in a downward spiral. Hanging on was killing him. Choosing my words carefully, I commented on the obvious pattern, but severing the connection was not his solution of choice.

Then, on the night of his sixty-fifth birthday, an interesting turn of events seemed to propel Carl forward in his healing. He invited a group of friends, including Nancy, over for dessert. After everyone else left, he and Nancy spent some quiet moments alone, reminiscing about old times. That night Carl went to bed feeling rather morose, and he had a series of distressing dreams with a repetitive theme. "In each dream I was lost," he said, "trying to find my way, unsuccessfully groping in the darkness for something to hang on to. I kept banging into things and getting hurt."

The following morning, Carl worked on some projects in his garage for a couple of hours. Shaking his head in exasperation, he said, "I was all fingers. It was as if everything I reached for was just beyond my grasp. I'd go to pick up a tool, miss it by an inch, and slam my hand into something else." The red marks on his knuckles told the story.

Carl was insightful, and I wondered aloud if he saw the thread woven throughout the incidents he had just described. He pondered the question, but nothing seemed to surface.

I offered a suggestion: "Could those dreams and your experience in the garage the next morning be expressions of the conflict you feel from trying to hang on to Nancy?"

Light dawned. After a few moments of quiet thought, he looked at me and said, "Yes. I believe that about hits the nail on the head."

19

The session ended shortly thereafter, and a month later Carl scheduled another appointment with me. This time he looked rested and stood an inch taller. I sensed his grief, but I also detected less agitation and a more forward focus. I commented on this and asked if he could identify what had made the difference.

He said, "I've quit grasping."

---

*An infant is born with a clenched fist,*

*but an old man dies with an open hand.*

*Life has a way of prying loose our grasp*

*on all that seems so important.*

ANONYMOUS

---

If we want to move successfully from one season of life to the next, at times we will have to release our grip on things past. And when we do, we must expect at first to experience intense and complex emotions. As endings, empty spaces, rifts, separations, and little deaths come our way, so do feelings of grief. When we are grieving such losses, it helps to know that God has good counsel for us. He hasn't left us hanging. Solomon penned these lovely lines, which are so much more than poetry:

20

There is a time for everything,
and a season for every activity under heaven:
a time to be born and a time to die,
a time to plant and a time to uproot,
a time to kill and a time to heal,
a time to tear down and a time to build,
a time to weep and a time to laugh,
a time to mourn and a time to dance,
a time to scatter stones and a time to gather them,
a time to embrace and a time to refrain,
a time to search and a time to give up,
a time to keep and a time to throw away,
a time to tear and a time to mend,
a time to be silent and a time to speak,
a time to love and a time to hate,
a time for war and a time for peace....
[God] has made everything beautiful in its time.
He has also set eternity in the
hearts of men.

ECCLESIASTES 3:1–8, 11

God has made everything *beautiful* in its time. Even the empty spaces. Even the holes. I admit that it's a hard concept for me to believe when I'm frantically grasping the last few strands of whatever is trying to escape my clutches. The pain involved in letting go doesn't feel "beautiful" to me; it feels downright miserable.

*21*

Yet in God's economy, new life springs forth from death. Jesus tried to help His followers understand this. His disciples had seen His triumphs. They had witnessed His miracles and experienced His power in their midst. They thought He was going to establish His kingdom on earth. Then one afternoon Jesus sat down on a hillside and told them that the time had come for Him to be glorified, but not in the manner in which they expected. Instead, it was to be by His death. And with tenderness and feeling, Jesus comforted them with an illustration:

> "The time has come for the Son of Man to be glorified. Listen carefully: Unless a grain of wheat is buried in the ground, dead to the world, it is never any more than a grain of wheat. But if it is buried, it sprouts and reproduces itself many times over. In the same way, anyone who *holds onto life* just as it is destroys that life. But if you *let it go*, reckless in your love, you'll have it forever, real and eternal.
>
> "Right now I am storm-tossed. And what am I going to say? 'Father, get me out of this?' No, this is why I came in the first place. I'll say, 'Father, *put your glory on display.*'"

JOHN 12:23–25, 27–28, *THE MESSAGE*, EMPHASIS MINE

Jesus bids us turn our eyes on the fields and observe the mature grain ready for harvest. He explains the process: no loss, no gain; no death, no new life. For Christ the analogy was very personal: His death was to become the gateway to life. Without His death, there would be no resurrection—for any of us.

The message is for you and me as well. It's a message of hope when life steals from us and leaves us with empty arms. It's a message of strength when we've been stripped bare and feel as though we're facing the future empty-handed. It's a message of substance that can fill the holes in our soul with a promise. God says to us:

> When you are letting go,
> remember that I am planting seeds of new life in you.
> Your grief is only for a season.
> My end is not death. It is always life.
> I am the author of life.[2]

These are the promises we have to hang on to when we are doing the hard work of letting go. Did you catch that? Letting go is hard work. It is often very bewildering. To break away from someone or something we have been bonded to rips at our emotions. It goes against our natural instincts. The parting cannot happen without inward bleeding. The greater the bond, the greater the pain.

Our head and our heart are usually in conflict. Our head says, *I need to do this for my own good. I need to let go because it's right. I need to let go because God is telling me to let go. I need to* let go for the sake of my kids or my spouse or my friendship or my own growth and development. But our heart says, *Oh, no you don't! It hurts too much. I can't do it. I won't do it!* Our logic and our emotions war with each other.

But there are some things we can do to cooperate with God in the process of letting go. We can take certain steps to help us move down life's path with a sense of curiosity and adventure, minus the claw marks. In the next chapter we will look at some of these steps.

*23*

---

*God does not leave us comfortless,*
*but we have to be in dire need of comfort*
*to know the truth of His promise.*
*It is in time of calamity…in days and nights*
*of sorrow and trouble that the presence,*
*the sufficiency, and the sympathy*
*of God grow very sure and very wonderful.*
*Then we find out that the grace of God is sufficient*
*for all our needs, for every problem,*
*and for every difficulty, for every broken heart,*
*and for every human sorrow.*

PETER MARSHALL

---

CHAPTER TWO

# RECOGNIZE

## THAT WHAT

S, IS

LETTING GO IS A PROCESS, NOT AN INSTANTANEOUS EVENT. It starts with an awareness of a difficult reality, and as our awareness increases, so does our pain. I once saw a poster that described the process perfectly. It was a cartoon of a woman whose head and arms were being squeezed through the wringers of an old washing machine. Beneath her anguished face the caption read, "The truth will set you free, but first it will make you miserable."

Facing the truth can be very difficult. Like surgery, acknowledging our disappointments and losses may hurt, but it can help move us toward wholeness. If we deny, block, stuff, or numb the pain, we end up camping out in our grief and never progressing beyond it. We cut ourselves off from the treasures God has hidden for us in the empty spaces, and we lock ourselves up emotionally.

As a counselor, I see this regularly in people like you and me. I'm talking about typical, get-up-in-the-morning-and-go-to-work, raise-the-kids kinds of people. Moms who help with PTA. Dads who coach Little League. Brothers. Sisters. Aunts. Uncles. Folks who seem normal on the outside but who are locked up on the inside.

Among them was Lori, a forty-six-year-old woman who told me about Matthew, the baby she had lost fourteen years earlier in stillbirth. "It's over," her family told her. "Forget it. Don't talk about it. We have to move on." And that's exactly what she did. She moved on, stayed busy, got involved in things, and kept her mind occupied. But Lori didn't move on emotionally. Her heart was tightly wedged in an incident long past. She was frozen in time, arrested in grief.

Matthew's name hadn't been mentioned since the day Lori left the hospital. There was no funeral, no memorial, no pictures, no discussion. Lori and her family treated the incident as if it had never happened. Cards sent by friends were burned unopened. The family thought that erasing the evidence would erase the pain.

But it didn't. It couldn't.

So now there were fourteen years of stockpiled pain. This was the way Lori handled other losses too. No wonder she was depressed. No wonder she felt as if she were about to burst. *The human heart was never designed to bury feelings alive.*

When Lori came to see me, she found the courage to recognize and face reality for the first time in fourteen years. Behind closed doors she gave herself permission to recognize her loss and talk about it—an important step in her healing. The denial was broken, and so was the power of the pain.[1]

*There is no power on earth more formidable than the truth.*

M  RGARET  LEE  RUNBECK

Then there was Marissa, who was skilled at keeping secrets—not because she wanted to, but because it was how she had learned to survive. Her father had sexually abused her from the time she was a little girl, and she didn't dare tell anyone. If she did, her father said, he would put her in jail and kill her mother. Little girls believe their big, strong daddies. In Marissa's innocent mind, there were no options. She had to be a good little girl. And part of being good was keeping the secret.

But the terrible secret, buried for so many years and landscaped with neat shrubbery and little flowers, became like a hidden toxic-waste dump. The poison seeped into the very soil of her life, gradually numbing and warping her soul, even the good parts. I saw evidence of the hidden toxins in her words:

"I want to enjoy my husband and kids,
but I have no feelings."

"It's as if I'm numb. Flat. I can't tell the difference between happy and sad."

"Nothing matters to me, even though I want it to matter."

"I used to be passionate and sensitive. I used to care. It's not like me not to care."

Again, we weren't built to bury our feelings alive. We weren't designed to deny our pain or to live by a "no talking" rule. The mind has limitations built into its defense system. If we block the bad, we also block the good. The result?

No sorrow…but no joy either.
No heartache…but no passion for life.
No grief…but no capacity for laughter.
It all gets locked up together.[2]

The good news is that there are keys to unlocking our pain, and they are right in our pocket. The first key is to recognize that what is, *is*. It is the essence of being brutally honest with ourselves and looking our painful truths in the face.

---

*Openness is to wholeness as secrets are to sickness.*

BARBARA JOHNSON

---

Sarah is a wonderful example of someone who courageously acknowledged her losses and let them go. Sarah came to our sessions impeccably dressed in the latest vogue, her makeup applied to perfection. But the eyes that stared at me were as cold and hard as chiseled marble. Sarah had struggled with an eating disorder for nearly twenty years, and she was one of the most bitter and controlling people I had ever worked with.

As we talked, I expected to uncover the source of Sarah's

bitterness. But the account of her childhood was rather typical and uneventful. No great traumas. No major heartbreaks. Her parents had a good marriage, and she spoke of a close relationship with both them and her two brothers. She butted heads with the boys now and then, as most kids do in the healthiest of families, but there was nothing out of the ordinary. Besides being blessed with parents who loved each other, she had the support of grandparents who lived next door. Her grandmother was like a second mom and confidante, especially during Sarah's teen years.

I was puzzled.

Sarah's family dynamics didn't fit the common profiles of patients with eating disorders. They weren't even close—no divorce, no abuse, no drugs or alcohol. Neither parent was intensely rigid, perfectionistic, or driven. They were churchgoing folk who took life in stride.

A piece of the puzzle was missing. It *had* to be.

Sarah recounted her years in high school and college in vivid detail. Cheerleading. Dance. Church choir. Gymnastics. Perfect grades. Scholarships. Sports awards. Titles. Then, in her third year of college, everything changed: Her grandmother died, and Sarah was raped. When she reached that point in her story, Sarah's reflections became blurred, and her account became fragmented.

That double-edged trauma became the hinge on which the rest of Sarah's life turned. The loss of her innocence and her confidante were more than she could bear, and, like an anesthetic, the eating disorder became her tool to numb the pain. Gymnastics and college became a thing of the past. The bubbly brunette with-drew from life and went into hiding—for *years*. Then, eighteen years later, she heard me speak in a conference about growing in hard places and made an appointment to see me.

Sarah spent several months in therapy, acknowledging and processing the trauma she had tucked away in secret. Facing the truth about her losses and how they affected her life gradually defused the power of her pain. Each week I saw change. At first tears and, eventually, spontaneous smiles broke through the barrier of her cold stares. Bit by bit, stone by stone, she dismantled the wall she had built around her heart and risked letting the pain out and letting others in.

In time, Sarah gained the courage to join a therapy group I facilitated for women in recovery. One night the group wanted to talk about "God issues" and how they perceived God's involvement in their lives. I passed out paper and markers and asked each woman to draw a picture that illustrated her rela-tionship with God.

One woman drew a stick figure of herself—no face, no hair, no clothes—kneeling on one side of a stone wall that towered high above her. Her face was buried in her hands. Bright sunlight shone on the other side of the wall, where Jesus stood with scores of other stick figures. She described herself as someone who was on the outside looking in. "I feel as if God has all kinds of friends down here on earth," she said, "but I'm not one of them."

As we went around the circle, each woman showed the others her picture. When it was Sarah's turn, she held up a like-ness of two very large hands holding the handles of an ornate vase. There were many colored markers she could have used, but she chose to do her picture strictly in black. The outline of the vase was carefully drawn and perfectly symmetrical. But down the middle of the vase she had drawn a thick, jagged line depicting a very deep crack.

Her description moved me. "This vase," she said slowly, "can't be fixed. The hands holding it are about to throw it away."

It wasn't a pretty picture, but even so, Sarah took a step forward that night. For the first time in eighteen years, she was truthful with herself and others about how she felt concerning her relationship with God.

I always marvel at God's sovereignty in putting groups together. One of the other members, Terry, immediately stepped in and asked Sarah *how* the vase had become cracked. Terry, herself a rape victim, happened to be nearing the end of her recovery. Within the safety of the group, Sarah was able to uncover the shame-filled events she had hidden for years. I had a front-row seat as I watched God do a deep work in Sarah through those women who offered her acceptance, grace, and truth.

Sarah's bitterness began to change in subtle ways. It didn't happen fast, but then long-term change rarely does. As the months passed, the eating disorder simply became less and less of an issue. Why? Because the pain driving her compulsion was losing its power. Sarah was learning to face her pain and let it go, so there was less need for an "anesthetic."

One day Sarah walked into my office and said, "I've made a decision. I want to be trained to work on the Rape Crisis

Hotline." She didn't want others to suffer in silence or live in denial, as she had for so many years. She wanted to be a refuge for those who were scared and hiding. She wanted God to use her brokenness to help others heal. She wanted others to know that there was hope.

Toward the end of Sarah's recovery, the group again raised "God issues." I had saved the pictures from the previous session and brought them out for review. Each of the women received a clean sheet of paper and colored markers, and when they were all finished, they showed the others their new drawings.

Sarah's new picture intrigued me. Guessing at its implications, I felt a surge of excitement. Once again she had drawn a perfectly symmetrical vase with swirly handles on the sides. Once again, the same two large hands firmly gripped it. The deep crack down the middle of the vase was still there too.

But Sarah had added something new. Using a fluorescent yellow marker, she had drawn heavy lines, like beams of light, spilling out of the fissure and flowing to the edge of the paper. Pointing to the crack she said, "*That's* where God shines through."

As the others reflected on her drawing, one woman said, "Hey, it looks more like a *trophy* than a vase to me."

"Yes!" said another who knew Sarah's story. "You're in God's hands. You're a trophy of His grace." The rest of the women nodded.

Once again I was reminded that it is through our suffering, our trials, and our wounds that God's glory is often

33

revealed. The caption under Sarah's picture could have read "2 Corinthians 4":

34

> For God, who said, "Let light shine out of darkness," made his light shine in our hearts to give us the light of the knowledge of the glory of God in the face of Christ. But we have this treasure in jars of clay to show that this all-surpassing power is from God and not from us. We are hard pressed on every side, but not crushed; perplexed, but not in despair; persecuted, but not abandoned; struck down, but not destroyed.
>
> Therefore we do not lose heart. Though outwardly we are wasting away, yet inwardly we are being renewed day by day. For our light and momentary troubles are achieving for us an eternal glory that far outweighs them all. So we fix our eyes not on what is seen, but on what is unseen. For what is seen is temporary, but what is unseen is eternal.
>
> 2 CORINTHIANS 4:6–9, 16–18

Unadorned clay pots. Vases with cracks. Earthenware jars with chips and dings and flaws. People with troubles, perplexities, weaknesses, traumas, and fear. That's all we are without God.

But *with* God...oh, we are so much more.

With God, we are people with a treasure inside, a treasure whose value is beyond price, reckoning, or comprehension. We are men and women with God's glory at work in us. His work doesn't entail removing our weaknesses or hardships. No, His work is displayed as He releases His divine power *through* our weaknesses.

*When life is hard and God is in us,* our broken places can become the windows where His glory shines through.

*When life is hard and God is in us,* we who are broken pots can become trophies.

*When life is hard and God is in us,* we can rest assured that somehow, in some way, He will bring His redeeming glory to bear in our lives and in the lives of others.

The longer I work with trauma victims, the more I am convinced that if a heart is open and truthful, there is *no* pain so deep or pervasive that God cannot heal it. And, as with Sarah, the broken places of our lives—the fractures, fissures, and jagged edges—can become the very locales where God's glory spills through in a torrent of light, hope, and healing. Out of our own personal darkness, God's penetrating light can touch those who still grope in the shadows.

Just ask one of the regulars on the Rape Crisis Hotline.

Her voice is strong, but softened by a deep compassion. The calls she receives on any given night vary wildly. But Sarah knows her assignment. She knows she's supposed to be there—just for those who need a glimpse of a strong and steady light penetrating the long night.[3]

36

*Let us not underestimate how hard*
*it is to be compassionate.*
*Compassion is hard because it requires*
*the inner disposition to go with others to the place*
*where they are weak, vulnerable, lonely, and broken.*

HENRI J. M. NOUWEN

## CHAPTER THREE

RELINQUISH
CONTROL
TO GOD

A NUMBER OF YEARS AGO I WAS INVITED TO SPEAK AT A major women's conference, but I couldn't help wondering why God even had me there, because He and I were in the middle of an intense power struggle.

Bottom line: I was pregnant for the fourth time, and I didn't *want* to be pregnant.

John and I were "finished having children," and it seemed to me that the Lord ought to have been well aware of that fact. We already had a daughter, Jessie, and a son, Benjamin. Our first baby was safe in heaven, and with one child of each flavor, we were balanced. Content. Comfortable. It was "us four and no more," and we loved it that way. We loved our ministry. Life was working out very nicely.

Then, out of the blue, I turned up pregnant.

How could it be? Well, I knew how it *could* be, but it shouldn't have been! We had taken all the necessary precautions. Somehow this baby was conceived in spite of the fool-proof birth-control method we had used for seventeen years.

I guess we didn't have as much control as I thought. Life

has a knack for teaching us that control is really an illusion.

At the time my emotions resembled a tossed salad—a wedge of guilt here, a slice or two of anger there, with some self-pity sprinkled over the top for spice.

*Guilt,* because I had friends who wanted so very much to get pregnant and couldn't, and here I was upset that the little test stick had turned blue.

*Anger,* because my agenda had been interrupted and rearranged.

*Self-pity,* because I was sick all day, every day, through most of the pregnancy.

One morning during the conference, I had some time off the platform, so I ordered breakfast in my room, read in the Gospel of John, and journaled my thoughts and feelings. I can assure you, God got an earful.

But then, after I had vented, it was *His* turn.

Through the years, the Lord has at times made some things very clear to me, and this was one of those times. As I was reading John 15, I came across a familiar passage that jolted me like a double dose of smelling salts. Jesus was speaking: "I am the true vine, and my Father is the gardener. He cuts off every branch in me that bears no fruit, while every branch that does bear fruit he prunes so that it will be even more fruitful" (John 15:1–2).

As I read those verses, I sensed God saying to me, *Pam, you're not being set back—you're being* cut *back.*

In that instant a picture of the three rose trees in our front yard came to my mind. Each summer the trees produce huge, yellow long-stemmed roses that fill our home with a glorious fragrance. Arranged in a vase on a table, the blooms seem to glow with a golden light of their own.

But in the fall, John cuts them back. *Way* back. After his pruning shears do the job, I look at those stumps and think, *My goodness, the man is ruthless. Those poor things look decapitated!* Every fall, I wonder if they'll ever grow back. But sure enough, every spring they do.

*Pam, you're not being set back—you're being cut back.*

In the quiet of that hotel room I knew that God was up to something in my life and that my pregnancy had in no way caught Him by surprise. For some incomprehensible reason, this was part of His plan to produce more beauty and fragrance in my life.

Ever so reluctantly, I waved my little white flag. *Okay, Lord*, I said. *I surrender to You.* That was no small first step! I wish I could say that it had been easier for me. How do you and I let go of the disappointments and losses we've suffered? We relinquish control. We surrender.

But not to "fate." Not to our emotions. Not to bitterness. No, we deliberately yield the controls of our life to God.

Oh, yes, it all sounds nice enough—and spiritual to boot. But, friend, surrender isn't always such a tidy bundle. Often it's a messy package of painful feelings like anger, rage, and deep sadness, which *eventually* give way to release and peace. As we surrender, we often feel frustrated and angry at God, at other people, at ourselves, and at life.

Oftentimes our saying *Yes, Lord*, simply opens the door to the grieving process. We suddenly find ourselves at the very

*The tendency is strong to say,*

*"…God won't be so stern as to*

*expect me to give up that!" but he will;*

*"He won't expect me to walk in the light so*

*that I have nothing to hide" but he will;*

*"He won't expect me to draw on his*

*grace for everything" but he will.*

OSWALD CHAMBERS

core of our pain and sadness: the heavy emotional burden that has to be released before we can feel right again. By allowing the grief to enter through the front door of surrender, healing can slip in, quiet and unannounced, through the back door.

Willpower isn't the key. Letting go is.

For many years I've heard men and women from all walks of life say things like:

- "I've invested too many years of my life trying to make people be what they don't want to be, or do what they don't want to do. I've driven them—and myself—crazy in the process."
- "I spent my childhood trying to make an angry father who didn't love himself be a normal person who loved me."

- "I've spent years trying to make emotionally unavailable people be emotionally present for me."
- "I've poured my life into trying to make unhappy family members happy, even though they don't seem interested in making the slightest effort."
- "I've given the last twenty-five years of my life trying to make my alcoholic husband stop drinking."

What they are all saying is something like this: "I've spent much of my life desperately and vainly trying to do the impossible and feeling like a dismal failure when I can't." It's like planting carrot seeds and trying passionately, creatively, and desperately to make those little plants grow prize tomatoes—and feeling defeated when it doesn't work.

By relinquishing control and surrendering to God, we gain the presence of mind to stop wasting time and energy trying to change and control things we can't change or control. Surrender gives us permission to stop trying to do the impossible and to focus on what is possible.

I wish I could say that surrender, letting go, is a one-time event. As I mentioned in the previous chapter, it's not. Yielding to the Lord is a continual, daily, sometimes hourly process. When God and I were locked in a wrestling match in that hotel room, it was only round one. Unbeknownst to me, down the road there were many more rounds to go.[1]

Less than three months later, our baby arrived, six weeks early and with a few surprises of his own. On the day Nathan was born, something was wrong. Terribly wrong. He was blue, not breathing well, and his little cry sounded muted. Instead of placing him in my waiting arms, the technicians scurried around trying to help him breathe. John held my hands, and we prayed for Nathan, asking God to help him and to guide the doctors' efforts.

I kept asking the nurses if Nathan was all right, but all I could get out of them was, "He's in good hands" and "They're helping clear his passageways." When I asked if I could nurse him, they said they didn't know. An hour later, impatient with vague answers and frustrated about being separated from my son, I asked the delivery nurse to wheel me into the care unit where they were working with Nathan. The pediatrician on call came over to talk with us. I didn't know this woman, and I didn't want to believe a word she was saying.

"Mrs. Vredevelt, your son is not oxygenating well, so we're trying to help him with oxygen and IVs."

"Is this life threatening?" I asked.

"It could be," she replied. "It's also my observation that he has Down syndrome. I've called a cardiologist to examine him because I think his heart isn't functioning properly."

At that point I wasn't tracking well and blurted out, "What does this mean?"

"It means he will be mentally retarded, Mrs. Vredevelt. There is also a higher incidence of leukemia for those with Down syndrome. There's a catheter in his heart, and the technicians are still working to stabilize him."

I spent that night alone in my room, listening to happy families around me celebrating their babies. My own doctor was in Russia. My pediatrician was on vacation. My parents were in California. John and the kids were home in bed, and a tiny boy named Nathan Vredevelt was in a sterile room under impersonal fluorescent lights, fighting for his life.

44

And me? I began to wonder just how much God really loved me. As hot tears rolled down my cheeks, I whispered into the night, *God, what is this? A bad joke? Well, I'm not laughing!*

The next morning, the cardiologist ran a battery of tests on Nathan. Based on the results, he said, the center section of Nathan's heart was not formed, and he would likely need open-heart surgery at the age of four months. During surgery, the doctor would construct the center portions of Nathan's heart so he could oxygenate better and grow more normally.

When the cardiologist left the room, wild and unchecked ruminations entered. *What if Nathan's heart fails and he doesn't make it four months? What if the surgery doesn't work? What if he gets sick and his body isn't strong enough to fight infection? How do we raise a child with Down syndrome? What if Jessie and Ben can't adjust to having a handicapped brother? What if...? What if...?*[2]

Round two of the wrestling match had begun.

Have you ever wrestled with God? Jacob did. Remember him? He lied to his blind, aged father and eventually stole his brother's inheritance rights—the most precious thing a man could possess. The name *Jacob* means "crafty deceiver," and Jacob tried hard to live up to his name.

Ah, but there came a night when this son of Isaac slipped through the ropes in the darkness and climbed into the ring with the angel of the Lord.

Jacob was left alone, and a man wrestled with him till daybreak. When the man saw that he could not overpower him, he touched the socket of Jacob's hip so that his hip was wrenched as he wrestled with the man. Then the man said, "Let me go, for it is daybreak."

But Jacob replied, "I will not let you go unless you bless me."

The man asked him, "What is your name?"

"Jacob," he answered.

Then the man said, "Your name will no longer be Jacob, but Israel, because you have struggled with God and with men and have overcome."

Jacob said, "Please tell me your name."

But he replied, "Why do you ask my name?" Then he blessed him there.

So Jacob called the place Peniel, saying, "It is because I saw God face to face, and yet my life was spared."

The sun rose above him as he passed Peniel, and he was limping because of his hip.

GENESIS 32:24-31

The text says that God allowed Jacob to prevail, but before He let His man up off the mat, He dislocated Jacob's hip. Let me assure you, friend: A dislocated hip isn't a hangnail or a bad-hair day. It's an extremely painful condition. And through all the years that followed, it was a constant reminder to Jacob that he was not to depend on his own strength. He was to rely entirely on God.

46

God loves us so much that He *will* wrestle with us. He's not going to give us everything we want all the time. That night when Jacob was alone in the dark, he wrestled with God—and God blessed his life. In spite of Jacob's seedy track record, in spite of his scheming, manipulative, and deceitful ways, God chose to open heaven's great storehouses and pour His favor out upon him. (Why does that encourage me so much?) From that point on, Jacob knew that his well-being was dependent on God's help, God's guidance, and God's blessing, not on his own devices. He gave up control.[3]

---

*The reason why many are still troubled,*

*still seeking, still making little forward progress,*

*is because they have not yet come to the end of themselves.*

*We are still giving some of the orders, and we are still*

*interfering with God's working within us.*

A. W. TOZER

---

It's a lesson about letting God be God—a lesson that I'll be working on every day until the Lord says it's time for me to exit this world and follow Him home.[4]

While we were in the hospital, the people in our church prayed for Nathan at a Wednesday evening service. That very evening his vital signs took a turn for the better. His oxygenation improved, and by morning the doctor was able to remove the IV from Nathan's heart. Four days later, during the Sunday morning services, the congregation prayed for Nathan again. This time they prayed specifically for the healing of his heart.

Mom flew into town to help us, and on the following Tuesday, she and I took Nathan to the hospital for more tests. The cardiologist wanted to examine all the cross sections of Nathan's heart on the ultrasound screen in order to determine how much of the heart muscle needed to be constructed.

We watched the screens intently as he focused on various chambers of the heart. When he got a clear shot of the center section, he started to shake his head and chuckle. Then in his clipped British accent, he announced happily, "By golly, the center of his heart is absolutely normal!"

I started to cry, my mom started to cry, and the doctor just kept shaking his head in amazement, muttering, "Very good, oh, *very* good."

Then he pointed to a small hole between the upper and lower chambers of the heart, showing us on the screen where the blood was spilling through. After taking some measurements, he consulted with us in his office.

"Mrs. Vredevelt," he said, "Nathan has two small holes in his heart. I want to watch them for the next six months and see if they will close on their own. If they do, surgery won't be necessary. If they don't, we'll need to patch them when he's a little older."

I cried, my mom cried, and the doctor beamed broadly, telling us how much he enjoyed giving good news. The presence of two small holes was much better news than any of us had expected. During the following six months, a host of friends around the country prayed for Nathan, and at his next appointment the cardiologist told us that the holes had closed. We no longer had to be concerned about surgery.

I left the hospital that day with a renewed awareness: God is still in the business of healing. That truth applies to baby boys with holes in their hearts and grown-up women with holes in their faith.

Either way, when we put everything in His hands, His is the touch that heals.

*The greatness of a man's power*
*is the measure of his surrender.*
WILLIAM BOOTH

## CHAPTER FOUR

REMEMBER

I'VE NOTICED SOMETHING ABOUT MYSELF AND PEOPLE IN general: When we have suffered disappointment and loss, our thoughts can easily wander onto a negative track. Grief distorts our perceptions. Emotional pain fuels faulty thinking and can bring on crises of faith. Pain skews judgment and can cause us to view reality with a pessimistic eye.

On the other hand, deliberately recalling God's goodness can lead us out of our discouraging doldrums. It's a good life strategy. That's what David, the writer of many of the Psalms, did when he was worn so thin that he didn't know if he could face another day in this world.

David, a man with a big heart and a tall assignment, knew well the highs and lows that come with life. His words reflect the anguish of his soul:

> I cry to the Lord; I call and call to him. Oh, that he would listen. I am in deep trouble and I need his help so badly. All night long I pray, lifting my hands to heaven, pleading. There can be

no joy for me until he acts. I think of God and
moan, overwhelmed with longing for his help.
I cannot sleep until you act. I am too distressed
even to pray!

Has the Lord rejected me forever? Will
he never again be favorable? Is his lovingkind-
ness gone forever? Has his promise failed? Has
he forgotten to be kind to one so undeserving?
Has he slammed the door in anger on his love?
And I said: This is my fate, that the blessings of
God have changed to hate.

PSALM 77:1-4, 7-10, TLB

But as we read further in the Psalm, something in
David's mood and tone does an about-face. Suddenly a song of
praise bubbles from the depths of his dark pool of despair:

O God, your ways are holy. Where is there any
other as mighty as you? You are the God of miracles and wonders! You still demonstrate your
awesome power.

What made the difference? What brought about the
change in David's heart? What washed away his grief?
Sandwiched between verses 10 and 13 is the key—the passage
in which David pauses and remembers. Here he recounts God's
faithful acts of love in his past:

I recall the many miracles he did for me so long
ago. Those wonderful deeds are constantly in my
thoughts. I cannot stop thinking about them.

PSALM 77:11–12, TLB

How about you? What do you do in those times of life
when you're so beaten down by demands that you're too tired
to pray? (By the way, lest you think you're all alone, I haven't yet
met a person who hasn't been there, including the woman I see
in the mirror every day!) What do you do when you feel as
though you're at the end of your rope and there's simply not
enough strength to keep holding on? What do you do when it
seems that the entire world is fighting against you?

David did something helpful: He remembered. He
listed all the times when God had made a difference in his past.

Everyone has experienced God's loving activity at a
pivotal moment in his or her life. I've had those moments.
You've had those moments. We may not have recognized them
every time, but God has been actively involved in our lives
from day one.

Think about it.

Have you ever had a narrow escape from a tough situation and felt that an invisible bodyguard had protected you?
Have you considered the possibility that God was the one that
rescued you?

Have you ever received a blessing you know you didn't
earn? God is the giver of all good gifts.

It is a delightful and profitable occupation
to mark the hand of God in the lives of ancient saints,
and to observe His goodness in delivering them,
His mercy in pardoning them, and His
faithfulness in keeping His covenant with them.
But would it not be even more interesting
and profitable for us to mark the hand
of God in our own lives?
Ought we not to look upon our own
history as being at least as full of God,
as full of His goodness and of His truth,
as much a proof of His faithfulness and veracity,
as the lives of those who have gone before?
Let us review our own lives.
Surely in these memories we will
discover incidents refreshing to ourselves
and glorifying to our God.

CHARLES SPURGEON

53

Have you ever steered away from trouble and toward something more noble because something inside you quietly craved purity? Only God makes people want to be holy.

Have you ever made a good decision that took you in a surprisingly positive direction just because you felt "led"? My hunch is that God was speaking to you.

Have you ever gone through a hard time, only to discover later that those difficult circumstances prepared you for something greater in your life? God is good at bringing something of great value out of adversity.

Many of us have probably discounted moments like these and considered them coincidence, luck, or a fluke. Or perhaps we celebrated some of these divine interventions but lost sight of them in the fog of the daily grind of life. The real question is not whether we have had moments when God intervened in our lives. The question is: What have we done with them?[1]

Remembering God's presence with me in the past gives me the faith and courage to handle the situations I face now. But how easy it is to forget! The memory dulls. We go to retrieve something from our mental files, only to find the cabinet locked.

Yet we must remember, because memories can beef up our courage. For years I've used the technique of recalling positive memories to empower my clients for peak performance. I've worked with a number of top collegiate athletes who struggle with anxiety, depression, and eating disorders. They need to prepare themselves mentally to compete, and as they anticipate an upcoming event, they have a choice. They can rehearse the times in their pasts when they made mistakes or major blunders and fell apart under pressure, or they can recall the times they operated at their optimal level. Which memories do you think have the ability to spur them to success?

If recalling positive memories enhances the performance of an athlete facing a challenging competition, imagine the difference it can make in building our faith for managing today's pressures and tomorrow's deadlines.

55

---

*Remind yourself that God is with you*

*and nothing can defeat Him.*

NORMAN VINCENT PEALE

---

It seems so simple. I suppose it is. Perhaps we try to make life too complicated and the solutions too difficult.

I think that, in some ways, our spiritual life becomes dwarfed when we forget our past. There is a propensity in our high-pressured, fast-paced society to allow the urgent demands of today and the worries of tomorrow to dominate our thinking. We live in the information age, and it's easy to jump to the conclusion that if we just gather more facts, secure more data, or run tighter calculations, our problems will be solved. But there comes a time when we need to stop seeking more information or advice and make remembering our prescription of choice.

When Nathan was born with Down syndrome, John and I went through a deep grieving process. We gathered information about the diagnosis, read book after book, and talked with specialist after specialist. We wanted to understand our son's condition to the best of our ability.

But stockpiling information didn't heal our pain. In fact, there were times when we didn't want to read another word or hear another thing from anyone about Down syndrome because the information that increased our awareness also fueled our fears. When we thought about our future of raising a mentally retarded son, we needed more than information. We needed some real-life, rock-solid reminders that God had not abandoned us. We needed some tangible reasons to hope. That's what remembering gives us.

Doesn't it make sense to build your faith on what you *do* know rather than on what you *don't* know? There are a lot of things I don't know. I don't know why Nathan was born with Down syndrome. I don't know why he hasn't been able to learn to talk. I don't know whether or not he will ever have the capacity to live and work on his own. Only time will tell. And I could spend a lot of time focusing on all the things I don't know and watch my faith erode. Or I can spend my time rehearsing what I know for sure.

I do know that God loves Nathan and has a plan and purpose for his life. I do know that Nathan has gifts and abilities that are allowing him to make valuable contributions to this world. I do know that though there are many difficulties and sorrows inherent in raising a child with a handicap, there are also many joys. Nathan is teaching us lessons about life and love that we probably would not have learned without him in our family.

How about you? What truths do your stories tell? When did God intervene in your past and help you survive losses and disappointments? If you need help remembering, just ask God. He can open your eyes and help you see a bigger picture.

57

Jesus said, "The Counselor, the Holy Spirit, whom the Father will send in my name, will teach you all things and will *remind* you of everything I have said to you" (John 14:26, emphasis mine).

Why? Because when our heart is burdened and we need encouragement, remembering matters.

Recalling empowers us.

Reflecting energizes us.

Reminiscing refreshes and restores our sense of balance.

---

*Remember that nothing is going to happen to you today that you and God cannot handle together.*

MILDRED WILLIAMSON

# CHAPTER FIVE

# RUN TO GOD

--- ✤ ---

RUN TO GOD. IT SOUNDS SO BASIC. BUT WHEN WE'RE IN pain, our first tendency is often to retreat from everyone, including God. We run in all kinds of directions by keeping ourselves excessively busy. We turn to activities, food, alcohol, novels, shopping, entertainment, and other people to mask our pain. Rollo May said it well: "It is an old and ironic habit of human beings to run faster when we have lost our way."

In our times of letting go, God is the one we need to run to because He knows us better than we know ourselves. He's the specialist who can give us insight into our needs. He's the chief guide who can offer direction when we're confused by the path before us. He's the caretaker of our souls who can give us strength and courage when we're afraid to let go.

Scripture provides a sturdy signpost when we find ourselves on a dangerous road:

> Trust in the LORD with all your heart and lean
> not on your own understanding; in all your

ways acknowledge him, and he will make your
paths straight.

PROVERBS 3:5–6

One of the best coping skills I know for dealing with the
painful realities of life is to tune your mind-set to watch for
God's activities. You'll find what you're looking for.

*61*

---

*There is rarely a complete silence in our soul.*

*God is whispering to us well nigh incessantly.*

*Whenever the sounds of the world*

*die out in the soul, or sink low,*

*then we hear these whisperings of God.*

*He is always whispering to us,*

*only we do not always hear*

*because of the noise, hurry, and distraction*

*which life causes as it rushes on.*

FREDERICK WILLIAM FABER

---

Look around you right now. Find five things that are the
color green or have green in them. With your mind-set tuned to
look for green, the color green will start to jump out at you.

Your eye will be drawn to a green shirt, a green book, leaves on flowers, a green notebook or pen. Have you ever noticed that after you've bought a new car, you begin to notice every other car like yours on the road? People find what they are looking for. If you're looking for conspiracies, you'll find them. If you're looking for God's perfect plan, you'll find it too.

When Nathan was diagnosed with Down syndrome, John and I were abruptly faced with the difficult assignment of letting go of many things we held near and dear to our hearts. We had to let go of our agenda for our lives, of our dreams for a healthy baby, of my professional position because much more of my energy was needed at home, of once-cherished areas of church involvement, of some of our free time, of my creative writing for five years, and of a few relationships due to lack of time and cultivation. It was a dark season of grief for all of us. But perspective arrived in an unexpected package one afternoon shortly after we brought Nathan home from the hospital.

I received a phone call from a friend. Knowing I had my hands full trying to adjust to so many changes, Kay said, "I'm coming over to clean your house. What's a good day?"

Kay showed up on my doorstep a couple of days later with our friend, Delight. What a sight greeted me when I opened the front door! These two looked like they had just stepped off the set of a science-fiction movie. They wore buckets on their heads, gas masks on their faces, combat boots, striped socks, and aprons over outfits that would have been rejected by the homeless.

They had come to make me laugh. And it worked!

Kay and Delight's visit was far more significant to me than the laughter—or the clean floors and dusted furniture they left behind. Kay is the mother of two, Kurt and Kara. We had known the family for many years because their son was in our youth group years ago when John and I worked with teenagers. Kara, their youngest, had been born with cerebral palsy and over the years had undergone extensive surgical procedures. For twelve years Kay had walked the path I was just beginning.

When I saw her standing there in that crazy getup on my porch, smiling from ear to ear, I remembered the many times I had seen her in the past and thought, *She has such burdens. How can she be so happy?*

I plopped myself in our big stuffed chair in the living room to nurse Nathan and said, "Kay, I'm struggling with something. I don't know how to view Nathan's handicap from God's perspective. How do you see it?"

Wise lady that she is, Kay didn't give me any platitudes or pat answers. Instead, she pointed me to Scripture. One of the passages that had been meaningful to her family since Kara's birth, she told me, was John 9. I had my copy of *The Message* at hand. Eager for some answers, I immediately picked it up and began to read:

> Walking down the street, Jesus saw a man blind from birth. His disciples asked, "Rabbi, who sinned: this man or his parents, causing him to be born blind?"

> Jesus said, "You're asking the wrong question. You're looking for someone to blame. There is no such cause-effect here. *Look instead for what God can do.*"

JOHN 9:1-3, *THE MESSAGE*, EMPHASIS MINE

Those verses gave me a fresh perspective that brisk fall afternoon. They challenged me to look for God in the midst of my daily grind. I resolved to quit trying to figure it all out and to believe that God would be working in our family as we made the adjustments needed to welcome Nathan.

*Look instead for what God can do.* I pondered those words for a long time as I held Nathan that day. I wondered how the blind man felt before Jesus came into his life. My hunch is that he assumed he would always be shrouded in darkness. Little did he know that he was headed for historical significance. Little did he know that one day he would stand boldly before the religious leaders of Jerusalem and testify to God's healing power in his life.

Who can give you and me the ability to believe that we have a future?

God.

Who can give you and me the faith to believe that our children are in God's hands—no matter what?

God.

Who can give us the faith to believe that God will have His way in our children's lives when circumstances seem to be pointing another direction?

God.

God challenges you and me to let go of our effort to make sense out of unexpected enigmas and to have eyes of faith for ourselves, our children, our marriages, our jobs, and our ministries. He says, "I know the plans I have for you.... They are plans for good and not for evil, to give you a future and a hope.... When you pray, I will listen. You will find me when you seek me, if you look for me in earnest" (Jeremiah 29:11–13, TLB).

God, with a full awareness of our weaknesses, wounds, handicaps, and disappointments, challenges us to run to Him. To place our trust in Him. Even when our hearts are breaking. Even when our logic screams that He doesn't care or that He has made a terrible mistake.

In the end, He will use us in His own special way. He will orchestrate our unique, divine assignments. And *nothing* can stop Him from achieving His purposes.[1]

In the midst of the pain and confusion that often accompany letting go, we need to run to God and say, *God, I need Your help. Give me Your perspective. Let my eyes see as You see. Let my heart hear Your heart. Grant me insight into what You are doing in my life right now. Show me what I need to do to cooperate with You in my healing.*

And then, dear friend, pay very close attention to the people who cross your path and the situations that present themselves. Be mindful of the insights that bubble to the surface and the whisperings of the Holy Spirit. Because God will be faithful to answer those kinds of prayers.

66

*If you keep watch over your hearts,*
*and listen for the voice of God and learn of Him,*
*in one short hour you can learn more*
*from Him than you could learn*
*from man in a thousand years.*

JOHANN TAULER

## CHAPTER SIX

RELEASE

THE

FEELINGS

PAINFUL EMOTIONS ARE BUILT INTO THE LETTING-GO process. No matter what we have to let go of, whether it's sending our youngest off to kindergarten or saying a final good-bye to our spouse of more than fifty years, we will feel grief. We will feel some degree of sadness, ambivalence, emptiness, anger, or confusion. These feelings aren't bad. They're normal, and it's necessary for us to feel them.

Time and again, psychiatric research has shown that an important part of letting go is *feeling*. Feeling leads to release. Denying, stuffing, or numbing our feelings with some sort of addictive behavior only prolongs and intensifies our grief. It blocks us from moving on in life.

I remember the ache in my empty arms after our first baby died halfway to term. With my postpartum hormones raging, the grief was more than I wanted to endure. At the counseling center one morning I said to a colleague, "I wish there were a pill I could take that would make these feelings go away."

He was very kind and, like a good friend, spoke the truth in love: "I can sure understand that, but then you would just have to work through your grief later."

He was making a point that I understand more fully now. Letting go demands that we feel and ride out our painful emotions. When we are feeling our pain, we are *progressing*. We tend to get mixed up about this process. We think that if we feel pain deeply, we are losing it, cracking up, or getting ready for the funny farm. Nothing is further from the truth. When we are feeling, we are moving ahead through the grief process.

I have a few statements I like to teach my clients:

Fish swim, birds fly, people feel.
Feeling is healing.
We get stuck in our pain not because we don't care, but because we don't give ourselves permission to feel.

In our book *Women and Stress,* Jean Lush and I share sixteen creative ways to release feelings constructively. [1] When we talk about managing emotions, we use a simple diagram of a storage pot. We are all storage pots. Scraps of emotion are collected in our pots: anger, jealousy, guilt, fear, joy, sorrow, excitement. In the process of letting go, all sorts of emotional scraps pile up in the pot. These scraps create tension. Our emotions are aroused, churning inside, and we begin feeling agitated, troubled, conflicted, tied up in knots, and out of sorts.

In the midst of this agitation, it's important to remember some basic truths of nature. First, tension is energy, and energy will always strive to be discharged. Discharge may come in a variety of ways, depending on our natural predisposition and choices.

Some people are fighters. They rarely close their lids. Whenever they are tense, they immediately unload their tension, regardless of the cost. They act out their emotions. Their rule of thumb is to find inner peace at any price. Fighters feel much better after blowing off steam, even though those around them may end up splattered on the pavement.

Other people are what I call "flighters." They have mastered the skill of sitting on the lid of their pot. Since the tension isn't discharged outwardly, it gets discharged inwardly. Flighters commonly suffer from psychosomatic illnesses and depression and engage in behaviors like avoidance and procrastination. Their motto is, "I must keep peace at any price."

When we have to let go of something important to us, we need to find ways to open some release valves, as we would on a pressure cooker, to let some of our emotional tension out in constructive ways.

One safe place to start is to talk to God—to tell Him about our hurt, our anger, our disappointment, and our sadness. Not for His sake, but for ours. He already knows the secrets of our hearts.

I'm not talking about prayers consisting of fancy, pious, religious words. I'm talking about authentically sharing our thoughts and feelings with God as we would with our most trusted friend. Whispers in the dark, cries from a lonely heart, sighs of confusion, and fumbling utterances offered to God will find their way to His ears. Some of the best prayers have more feelings than words.

*Prayer is more than words.*
*It's listening, seeing, feeling.*

NORMAN VINCENT PEALE

I've seen powerful breakthroughs when people invite the healing presence of God into their place of brokenness. Some of the most effective therapy occurs when people talk to God in prayer. As they share their pain with Him, healing happens. When they have suffered terrible losses and gross injustices, logic and pat answers don't defuse their pain. Releasing their grief does.

I've seen it in my own life. The morning after our son was diagnosed with Down syndrome, I consulted with a physician in my hospital room. Still reeling from the news of my baby's condition, I looked at him and asked, "How did this happen?"

He did what he was supposed to do. He gave me the scientific explanation for Down syndrome and Nathan's heart problems and tried his best to comfort me. I'll never forget his closing comment: "Mrs. Vredevelt, it was just a chromosomal anomaly, a genetic mishap, *a mistake.*"

I know that this man sincerely felt bad for me and that he wanted to alleviate any guilt I might have felt at the time. The "whys" of medical crises are sometimes as baffling to doctors as they are to patients. I was grateful for the compassion I saw in his eyes.

But when he left, I didn't know what to do with the information he'd given me.

A *mistake? Whose* mistake?

I propped myself up with a few pillows and sat there in a stupor, overwhelmed by a mishmash of thoughts. Defending myself against the pain, I intellectualized the ordeal. *Okay, Pam, this is how it works. You live in an imperfect world, and your body isn't perfect. Your body made the mistake. Or perhaps the mistake occurred during the process of conception.*

Logic didn't heal the pain. It rarely does.[2]

No, it's when we are open and honest about our thoughts and feelings in safe relationships that healing comes. First Peter 5:7 says, "Cast all your anxiety on him because he cares for you." The word *cast* is a very aggressive term that means "to throw off."

Intellectualizing and using logic as a defense against my pain didn't facilitate healing. It was only as I openly shared my thoughts and feelings with God—and purged the pain in my soul within the safety of His healing presence—that comfort came.

In the Psalms we see that David mastered the art of throwing his pain onto the Lord in prayer. He didn't censor his feelings. He didn't carefully weigh his words. He didn't try to pretend things were fine when they were awful. Nothing was sugarcoated. David was brutally honest about his feelings as he poured out the depths of his heart to God:

> Open your ears, God, to my prayer;
> don't pretend you don't hear me knocking.
> Come close and whisper your answer.
> I really need you....

My insides are turned inside out....
I shake with fear,
I shudder from head to foot.
"Who will give me wings," I ask—
"wings like a dove?"
Get me out of here on dove wings;
I want some peace and quiet....
Haul my betrayers off alive to hell—let them
experience the horror, let them
feel every desolate detail of a damned life. I call to God;
God will help me.
At dusk, dawn, and noon I sigh
deep sighs—he hears, he rescues....
Pile your troubles on God's shoulders—
he'll carry your load, he'll help you out.
He'll never let good people
topple into ruin.

PSALM 55:1–2, 4–6, 15–18, 22, *THE MESSAGE*

Did you know that two-thirds of the Psalms are songs of lament? Time and again we see a pattern in this very human book of poetry: David comes to the Lord in anguish and vents his deepest feelings, but by the end of the Psalm, he sees things from a fresh perspective of hope.

Prayers of ventilation will allow you to release your feelings constructively. Journaling can help too. You can write uncensored thoughts, free-flowing feelings, and letters to the Lord about what's going on in your inner world.

And give yourself permission to cry. Don't try to keep a stiff upper lip. God gave us tear ducts for a reason. Tears cleanse the soul. Whenever I counsel people who are grieving, I encourage them to carve out times when they can have a good, hard cry and express their sadness fully. But I also encourage them to place some limits on that expression. I suggest that after some deep sobbing, they make themselves a cup of tea, take a bath, go for a walk, or scrub their kitchen floor to purposely divert themselves from their pain for a while. The key is full expression—within limits.

Why limits? Because we can work ourselves into a neurotic mess if we give full vent to negative feelings for hours at a time. One of the reasons therapy sessions are limited to about fifty minutes is because if they are much longer, clients get weary and recovery work is less than effective. Freedom with containment is the key.

I saw a refreshing authenticity in Nancy as she picked up the pieces of her life after learning of her husband's affair. She had suspected the betrayal for quite some time but discounted the warning signs and shamed herself for being suspicious. His confession blew her world apart. Resentment and bitterness smothered her. She seriously wondered if she would ever be able to dig her way out from under these realities. I'll let Nancy tell her story:

> I remember reading the Bible and wondering
> where God was in this mess. I read stories of
> God's healing and grace and thought, *What a*

RELEASE THE FEELINGS

*crock! These words must have been written by people who were out of touch with reality.*

It was hard for me to trust anyone, much less God. I did a fine job of protecting myself from Him and everyone else with a shield of angry detachment. The only one I allowed anywhere near my heart was my best friend, Karen.

75

Karen stayed close in this dark valley. She prayed for me each day. She talked about God's love and about her high hopes for my future. She listened to me. She cried with me. She did not judge me. And she didn't tell me what to do.

During our separation, Doug visited the children periodically for a few hours at a time. Our kids were broken by the sorrow of our fragmented marriage and the uncertainty of the ongoing separation. I was barely able to function under the stress of the changes. I think the only reason I kept going was because I felt the deep need to relieve the children's pain. It was strictly for their sake that I reached out to others and persevered.

These were dark years that caused me to take inventory. I took a long, hard look at me. I remember crying in a heap on the bathroom floor, asking God to change me. I begged Him for strength to cope with the bone-crushing weariness that came from my unrelenting efforts to hold our family together. Eventually the blinders were lifted from my eyes, and I could see that I was absolutely powerless over Doug's choices.

I also asked God to heal the pervasive suspicion and fear that had consumed me. Healing began when I was completely honest and said, *God, I don't trust You, but I see people who do and I want to.* Even though fear distorted my picture of reality, I knew deep down that God was the only one who had the answers that I could not find within myself.

---

*Do not let it be imagined that one must remain silent about one's feelings of rebellion in order to enter into dialogue with God. Quite the opposite is the truth: it is precisely when one expresses them that a dialogue of truth begins.*

PAUL TOURNIER

---

For several years, though, it seemed as if I had lost my way with God. I continued to wonder if there was something terribly wrong with me and if somehow Doug was justified in his choices. I filed for divorce and remained silent about Doug's infidelity. People questioned me. They asked why I couldn't forgive him. Surely, they thought, we could have worked things out.

But they didn't know the whole story, and frankly, I didn't think it was any of their business. Trying my best to go on without Doug, I slammed the door shut on the guilt over filing for divorce and the unresolved grief over losing our family.

I had long, angry talks with God. I raged. I asked Him where He was when my husband was betraying me. Why hadn't He protected me and the children from this abuse? I told Him how desperately unsafe I felt in this God-forsaken world. I wondered about the next shoe He planned to drop.

All the while, God listened patiently and continued sending blessings that were difficult for me to see through the dense fog of my grief.

I was so overcome with the injustice the children and I had suffered that I wanted Doug to pay. Vengeance seemed like a practical and logical solution. If I just opened my mouth and told all, I could have destroyed him.

But something constrained me. Actually, Someone constrained me. The Spirit of God began to speak to me about letting go of my bitterness. Everywhere I turned, somebody was saying something about forgiveness. The lady on *The Oprah Winfrey Show.* The song on the radio. The preacher at church. My friend on the phone. They were all delivering the same message: "Forgive."

*Forgive?* I cried to God. *Impossible! How do you forgive people who don't deserve forgiveness?*

"You pray for them."

*But, God, I don't want to pray for Doug. I don't want to pray for his sideline attractions. They betrayed me. I will hate them forever!*

"Not if you pray for them."

It was about the time that this war was going on in my head that Karen gave me Dr. James Dobson's book *When God Doesn't Make Sense,* which explores the subject of suffering unjustly. As I read, the doctor brought me face-to-face with a set of choices. I could either continue my descent into bitterness and resentment, or I could turn to God. Neither choice seemed very appealing.

I wrestled with these ideas for months before I was able to bring myself to tell God that I couldn't let go on my own. A gratifying sense of power came from holding on to my anger and resentment. There was a part of me that wondered if I would crumble if I released it. I needed God to give me supernatural strength to do what He had asked me to do: pray for those who had betrayed me.

Moments of fleeting relief came as I journaled my uncensored feelings in a daily diary. Revealing the most intimate details of my life helped purge the pain. I read about a man named Job who was able to put words to the anguish I was feeling. I found solace in his life story and in the fact that God was the one who had the final word in his life. Not his friends. Not his family. Not his acquaintances. It gave me hope to know that God's last word in Job's life was one of total restoration.

It is true that the injustices I suffered from my husband's sexual addiction stole my sense of worth and personal dignity. But looking back, I can see that the bitterness I hung on to for several years robbed me of the ability to heal and move forward. A turning point came when I realized that I could not afford to leave unchecked the hatred simmering in my heart.

I had to acknowledge that what happened to me *happened.* I was not crazy. My children and I bore the scars of a terrible injustice. But denial was not the answer. Neither was amnesia or sugarcoating the truth. I had to face the facts and grieve the reality of the injustice if I was ever going to be able to move beyond it. I knew I couldn't keep trying to cover the cracks in my heart for the rest of my life.

Somewhere along the line, I heard someone say that if we all lived by the rule "an eye for an eye," the whole world would be blind. It reminded me of the many mistakes I had made in my life and of God's unending compassion and grace to forgive me. How could I not forgive when God had forgiven me of so much? I made a conscious choice to let go of my quest for justice for Doug and the women who had betrayed me.

I felt nothing. But I did what I knew God had told me to do months before. I prayed for them and released them into God's hands. I decided that from that day forward it wasn't my job to set them straight or to make them pay. Their wrongs were between them and God. My energies were going to be focused on my own health and the well-being of my children.

To this day I have moments when the past, with all of its hurts and memories of failure, sweeps in like a raging river and leaves me gasping for air. I visit the pain every so often, but I no longer live in it. I am now one of those stories of hope that I used to read about while consumed with anger.

I'm convinced that nothing will kill a woman's spirit faster than holding on to resentment. And nothing will dissolve bitterness more effectively than choosing to let go and forgive. Forgiveness doesn't come easily, and believing it does will likely ensure that we never forgive. If we call a spade a spade, forgiveness is often unattainable from a human standpoint. But when you factor in the divine, all things are possible. God can supernaturally empower us to release our death grip on rage and let it go. We simply have to say, *God, I'm willing to be made willing*.

I told the Lord several years ago that I was willing. And from then on I began to sense that God was touched by my pain, that He had taken up my cause, and that He held both me and Doug in His hands. He would have the final say in both of our lives. Eventually I embraced the peace that only God could give. The pain of abandonment will probably never go away, because we suffered many severe losses. But the girls and I have moved on with our lives, and while we grieve our losses, we are no longer controlled by them. There is life beyond Doug. And it's a good life, blessed by God.

If we want to snip the soul ties that keep us in bondage…

If we want to take back the dignity that has been stolen from us…

If we want God to heal the holes in our souls…

If we want to douse the flames of bitter revenge…

If we want something good to come out of something very, very bad…

…we must take the steps of healing.[3]

We must recognize that what is, is and not avoid or rationalize away our losses. We must relinquish control to God with full awareness that He is God and we are not. And we must experience and release our feelings. Feeling is healing.

Life requires us to let go, over and over and over again. Letting go doesn't eliminate our loss, but it reduces unnecessary suffering. As we do our part, God will *always* do His. When we release our grip and open our hands to Him, we give Him a new place to deposit whatever we need to move us forward in our healing.

---

*Pain and pleasure are opposites:*

*when you share grief, you decrease it;*

*when you share joy, you increase it.*

ANONYMOUS

---

## CHAPTER SEVEN

REVISIT

THE

BASICS

I BUCKLED MYSELF INTO THE SEAT, GLANCED OUT THE window of the plane, and checked my watch. *So far, so good.* We were departing on schedule. The flight attendant welcomed us aboard and gave the usual instructions. "In the event that the cabin loses pressure, an oxygen mask will fall from the compartment above you. Slip the mask over your nose and mouth and breath normally. If you are traveling with children, or someone is seated next to you who needs help, put your own mask on first and then help others."

I had heard the statement hundreds of times before, but this time something about it struck a dissonant chord in me. The thought crossed my mind that my natural reaction would be to want to help my children first. No doubt that's why they give the instructions. The authorities are well aware of a parent's instinct to protect, and they also know that a child requires less oxygen than an adult. If adults pass out from oxygen deprivation, they aren't going to be of any help to children.

Now and then I observe a paradox among those who serve others: caretakers who don't take care of themselves. Many people I talk with in my counseling office or at conferences regularly place their own needs at the bottom of their to-do list. The job, the boss, the kids, the spouse, the community, the church—everyone else gets the best they have to offer. The caretakers get the leftovers, as if everyone's life except theirs deserves attention and support. The tragic result is that these caring folks end up living life on the verge of burnout.

85

---

*You will break the bow if you keep it always bent.*

GREEK PROVERB

---

While talking with Carmen during a therapy session, I learned that she had been the primary caretaker of her ailing parents for ten years. She nursed her father for four years before he died. Shortly after he passed on, her mother had a stroke, and Carmen spent the next six years attending to her needs. Not surprisingly, after her mother's death, Carmen felt like she was "caving in." The loss of her beloved parents was intensely painful, but exhaustion further complicated the grief. When I asked Carmen about the nature of some of her own needs, her eyes glazed over into a blank stare. "I don't know," she sighed. "I really haven't thought about it." Together, we set out to help her think about it and learn the basics of healthy self-care.

Grief is hard work. It takes emotional energy to let go of something near and dear to our hearts. When we're processing a painful loss, it's important to give ourselves permission to down-shift into survival mode, to streamline our activities and conserve our mental and emotional resources. We typically don't have much of an emotional buffer when we're in the throes of a major life adjustment. That's why self-care is critically important.

---

*If you don't slow down, you'll break down.*

JUDITH ST. PIERRE

---

Revisiting the basics is a good place to start. It's amazing how symptoms of anxiety and depression are diminished by incorporating three simple ingredients into our routine: healthy meals, ample sleep, and regular exercise. They provide a firm foundation for successfully letting go. If we subtract one or more of these three components from the equation, we run the risk of arresting, or at least inhibiting, our forward movement in life.

Think about it. Have you ever noticed that when you are in a time of transition, your eating, sleeping, and exercise habits tend to become somewhat erratic? Transitions are stressful. When stress increases, compulsions also increase, and routine tends to be less than consistent. We find ourselves eating more (or less) than necessary, grabbing junk food on the run, or skipping meals altogether. Our sleep patterns can become erratic. We may sleep more than usual, lay awake at night, or burn the candle at both ends. Likewise, we may cut back on exercise, skip it altogether, or become more compulsive about it.

Let's revisit these basics, one by one, and examine ways to manage them during the letting-go process.

There are many helpful books that offer sound eating

programs, so I don't want to go into great detail here, but I do want to underline the importance of consistently eating nutritious food. For some, that means three balanced meals a day. For others, depending on their energy output and blood-sugar sensitivities, it may mean four or five small meals a day.

During a season of letting go, what you eat can make a significant difference in your endurance. Letting go of disappointment and painful losses requires high-octane fuel. Diet soda and junk food aren't going to give you what you need when you're mentally and emotionally taxed by chronic stress. Some nutritional experts suggest increasing your protein intake at such times because protein is a stabilizing energy source that burns longer than carbohydrates. Adding a high-quality vitamin-mineral supplement can also bolster the body during prolonged periods of stress.

In the year following Nathan's birth, I was physically and mentally exhausted from adjusting to the reality of his handicaps, illnesses, sleepless nights, and the fluctuating hormones in my postpartum body. I had to force myself to eat three healthy meals a day. I had no creative energy for cooking fancy meals, so I had to simplify everything. The objective was to get something from each of the five food groups (meat, dairy, fruit, vegetable, and starch) every meal. I relied on simple cuts of meat, convenience foods, and recipes that were quick and easy to prepare. During that year, we barbecued on the gas grill several times a week and frequently used the rice cooker. Fruit, nuts, and protein bars provided quick, energy-boosting snacks between meals.

While I'm sure there were days when I didn't hit my objective, at least I had a target to shoot at. Remember the old saying: If you aim at nothing, you're sure to hit it. On days when I was more disciplined and stuck with the program, my stamina was significantly better, and there was a marked difference in my emotional energy.

Sleep is another of our most important needs when we're in the process of letting go. I remember talking with a mother whose eleven-month-old baby had died after complications from surgery. "All I want to do is sleep," she complained. While it's a fact that one of the red flags of depression is wanting to sleep more than necessary, I was puzzled by her remark. After her baby died, she had taken a full-time job and was putting in ten-hour days as an executive assistant. I asked her how much she slept, and she said, "From 9 P.M. to 7 A.M.," as if this were a ridiculous amount of time to be in bed.

It had never crossed this woman's mind that she needed the extra sleep because of the heavy emotional burden she was bearing—not to mention the stress of learning a new job! From my perspective, those ten hours of sleep didn't point to pathology; they indicated good self-care. The body needs time to restore and replenish itself when we are carrying heavy emotional loads.

"For those who are suffering with symptoms of anxiety and depression, I'm going to save you $120 right now," I said to a group of professionals gathered for a stress-management conference. "You can significantly reduce these symptoms by getting eight to nine hours of sleep a night."

*Sleep is God's celestial nurse who croons*
*away our consciousness, and God deals*
*with the unconscious life of the soul in places*
*where only He and His angels have charge.*
*As you retire to rest, give your soul and*
*God a time together, and commit your life to*
*God with a conscious peace for the hours of sleep,*
*and deep and profound developments will*
*go on in spirit, soul, and body by the kind*
*creating hand of our God.*

OSWALD CHAMBERS

As I expected, people fidgeted in their seats, smirked, glanced around, and gave me *the look*. You know, the look that says, "Yeah, right, lady! What planet do you live on?" Of the several hundred gathered in the room that day, very few raised their hands when I asked, "Who averages eight to nine hours of sleep a night?"

We live in a fast-paced world, constantly struggling to meet its unending demands. We work, raise families, build marriages, tend to friendships, and try to cram in some exercise and recreational activities. Our daily planners are full of to-do lists. There are never enough hours in a day to get it all done.

A friend of mine recently had his gall bladder removed. As a corporate executive, he was used to having a lot of energy and maintaining a high level of productivity, but recuperating was taking its toll. When he complained to his doctor that he was still feeling tired two weeks after the surgery, his doctor said, "Following this type of surgery, the body heals at a rate of 15 percent per month from the inside out—*if* a person rests and takes good care of himself. If you push too hard, you'll delay your recovery."

When we suffer a major disappointment or a difficult loss, it's as if part of who we are is surgically severed or cut away. It takes time and rest to recover. Sleep is one of the primary ways the body restores itself. If we rob ourselves of it through overactivity, we slow our recovery and impair the healing process. In short, we prolong and intensify the pain involved in letting go.

---

*Activity itself proves nothing:*

*the ant is praised, the mosquito swatted.*

ANONYMOUS

---

My grandfather, an entrepreneur and successful businessman, used to say, "The only problem with sleep is that you've got to take it lying down." He was a hard-working man who could close his eyes and catch a few winks just about anywhere and then awake refreshed for the rest of the day. These catnaps were in addition to the solid eight hours of sleep he got at night. It's a model of self-care worth considering.

We're more likely to be successful in our endeavors of letting go if we lay aside our to-do lists and put ourselves to bed in a timely fashion. With refreshed minds and healthy bodies, we'll be more effective in handling the new list tomorrow.

91

---

*I found I could add nearly two hours*

*to my working day by going*

*to bed for an hour after lunch.*

SIR WINSTON CHURCHILL

---

Finally, when you're doing the hard work of letting go, exercise is prescriptive, not optional. Although I'm not an expert in physiology, as a clinical counselor I know the mental and emotional benefits of exercise. Studies have shown that exercise is a key to managing depression and anxiety. It's a cheap, easy way to elevate mood, decrease agitation, and deliver a sense of calm to the brain. The endorphins released during aerobic exercise, for example, are powerful mood elevators and natural tranquilizers. Exercise is also a superb tool for managing anger. When we exercise, we physically force tension out of our bodies.

For as long as I can remember, exercise has been a part of my routine. I used to swim a mile on my lunch hour. After my children were born, I had less time and energy for the pool routine, so I started walking—something I still do today. When the weather is nice, I enjoy walking the hills in our neighborhood for thirty to sixty minutes, four or five days a week. If it's pouring rain, a treadmill comes in handy. While I do have to carve out time in my schedule for walking, I think I probably save time in the long run. My proficiency on task is much better when my mood is good, my mind peaceful, and my body strong. The more hectic and pressured a week becomes, the more I need my "sanity walk" to defuse the tension, restore calm, and help me sleep deeply at night.

The most frequent rebuttal I hear to the argument for exercise is that it just takes too much time. But exercise for enhancing our emotional state really requires only thirty to forty minutes, several times a week. We don't have to spend long hours in the gym. Some experts say that maintaining a consistent training-level heart rate for twenty-five minutes will alter the brain chemistry in much the same way that an anti-depressant does.

I encourage my clients to set aside a minimum of thirty minutes for any aerobic activity, since it takes a few minutes to work the heart up to a training-level pulse. An exercise trainer at a local club can help you calculate your training heart rate based on your age and overall physical condition.

For me, the benefits far outweigh the cost. In fact, when I don't exercise, I pay for it. I'm more irritable, little things get to me, and I find myself reacting to life in ways I don't want to.

If you are in the middle of transition, struggling emotionally with deep disappointment or painful loss, I sincerely hope you will set aside time for exercise. It really doesn't matter what kind of activity you choose, as long as it's aerobic and increases your heart rate and the flow of oxygen and blood to the brain. Do something you enjoy. Walk. Ride a bike. Swim. Jog. Rollerblade. Play an intense game of basketball. Any activity is worthwhile if it pushes the tension out of your body and releases the natural chemicals in the brain that help you cope.

93

*Renewal and restoration are not luxuries. They are essentials. There is absolutely nothing enviable or spiritual about a coronary or a nervous breakdown, nor is an ultra-busy schedule necessarily the mark of a productive life.*

CHUCK SWINDOLL

When we are doing the hard work of letting go, we can assist the process by downshifting into survival mode and getting back to the basics. Taking care of ourselves isn't selfish—it's smart. If we are tending to our own needs, we are more likely to have something worthwhile to offer others. Jesus said, "Love your neighbor as yourself" (Luke 10:27). Our effectiveness in loving others begins with a choice to love ourselves. When we fill ourselves up first, we're more likely to have something worthwhile to pass on to another. As every flight attendant reminds us, it's impossible to offer others oxygen if we've ceased breathing ourselves.

94

*Prescription for a happier and healthier life:*
*Resolve to slow your pace;*
*learn to say no gracefully;*
*resist the temptation to chase after more*
*pleasures, hobbies, and more social entanglements;*
*then "hold the line" with the tenacity of*
*a tackle for a professional football team.*

DR. JAMES DOBSON

# CHAPTER EIGHT

# REVISE

# EXPECTATIONS

THEY SAY YOU GET WHAT YOU EXPECT. BUT THEN, WHAT DO "they" know anyway?

Launi expected to be married happily ever after. It didn't happen.

Tammy, Jackie, Martin, and Len expected their partners to be faithful. They weren't.

Bob and Dave expected their company revenues to increase 25 percent last year. Instead, they both filed for bankruptcy.

Karen and Phil expected their son to go to college in the fall. He died in a motorcycle accident this spring.

Dace, Mira, Judy, and I expected to give birth to healthy babies. Yet each of us has a child with special needs.

An Old Testament gentleman named Job had some expectations, and he too felt the bone-deep ache of disappointment when they didn't come about. At one point he admitted, "When I expected good, then evil came; when I waited for light, then darkness came" (Job 30:26, NASB).[1]

This morning I went for a sanity walk with a friend. She is a faithful, devoted mother of four children who has known the deep disappointment of unrealized dreams. "From the time my kids were little, I expected them to finish high school, attend college, and start families," she told me. "I didn't have any lofty dreams that any of them would be the president of the United States or the first astronaut to set foot on another planet. I just expected the basics.

"My husband and I were devastated when our oldest son started experimenting with drugs and dropped out of high school. Even though we had taught him well about the dangers of substance abuse, he chose to ignore us and go his own way. When our second son fathered a child out of wedlock, our expectations were shattered all over again. We had hoped that grandchildren would come along after the children were married, not before. Things didn't turn out anything like we had expected, and letting go of the dreams we had for our boys has been one of the most painful experiences we've ever endured."

"So how did you do it?" I asked her. "How did you let go?" It was obvious to me that, for the most part, she was on the other side of the debilitating grief, no longer incapacitated by the pain. I wondered what had helped usher her to that place of peace.

She referred me to a story in the Bible. "Do you remember the story of Abraham and Isaac?"

I nodded, for I knew the story well.

"Do you remember how Abraham placed Isaac on the altar and offered him up to God?"

"Yes," I replied, seeing the image in my mind.

"Well, that's what I had to do. As clearly as if it happened yesterday, I remember when, years ago, I cupped my hands in front of me, pictured my boys in my palms, and lifted them up to God. I told Him, *I place my boys in Your hands. They're Yours. You take over. Please fulfill Your plans for their lives.* I realized that our job of helping direct their course was done, because they were not open to our input.

98

"From that point on our expectations changed. We decided that we would do our best to love and support the boys in practical ways, but that the results were between them and God."

I thought about my friend's words and the many times I too had placed my children in God's hands. I'll probably be praying those kinds of prayers until the Lord decides it's time for me to come home. It hurts to see your kids struggle and take hard knocks. For me, comfort comes from knowing that grasping, clinging, and hanging on with white-knuckled fists doesn't help. But letting go, and placing whatever is troubling me into God's loving care, does.

As an approach to meeting our needs, letting go is very different from clamping down, striving, and trying harder.

Not long ago, I was sitting in my counseling office with a client who was confused and conflicted about a number of things going on in her life. In passing, she mentioned that she had attended a funeral for a little boy with Down syndrome who had died of leukemia. She didn't know that my son was handicapped or that when Nathan was born, we were told there is a higher incidence of leukemia among those with Down syndrome than there is for the typical population. She had no idea what strong emotion her story stirred in me.

For the moment, I did the clinical thing. I suppressed

the emotion and focused on helping my client. But as most of us know, suppressed emotion doesn't stay down for long. It's like trying to hold a beach ball under water. No matter what you do, it keeps popping up.

I succeeded in pushing this woman's story to the back of my mind until the next evening, when I was sitting by the fire reading my mail. Among the stack of papers, there was a letter from a woman who had read my book *Angel Behind the Rocking Chair*. She recounted some of the beautiful characteristics of her son, whom she had recently lost after a long battle with leukemia. The child had had Down syndrome and was Nathan's age.

Well, that did it. I was overcome with emotion. All the feelings of the previous day came flooding back. At such times, one thing is certain: No amount of striving or trying harder is going to resolve those deep conflicts of the soul.

I went to my bedroom, sat on the bed, had a hard cry, and talked to God. I told Him about my fears and asked Him to help me live in the here and now and not to forecast negatively into the future. And then I said something I don't think I had ever formally said before: *God, I choose to trust You with Nathan's life and with Nathan's death.* It was a statement of letting go that ushered in a sense of peace. My emotions weren't at flood stage anymore. They had subsided.[2]

Recently I came across a Scripture that spoke to me about suffering and expectations:

Then [Jesus] told them what they could *expect* for themselves: "Anyone who intends to come

with me has to let me lead. You're not in the
driver's seat—I am. Don't run from suffering;
embrace it. Follow me and I'll show you how.
Self-help is no help at all."

LUKE 9:23-24, *THE MESSAGE*, EMPHASIS MINE

As card-carrying members of the human race, we
should expect suffering. Expect heartache. Expect pain and disappointment. Expect the unexpected. Yet while all this is true,
we can also expect that as we give God the lead, He will give us
what we need to endure the heartaches we experience. He will
show us how to navigate the raging storms that come our way.

I recall taking our children to a pediatrician for check-
ups and being told that they needed immunizations. The nurse
explained the risks and ramifications of the shots and quoted
some statistics. One out of an astronomical number of children
experiences adverse reactions, she said. This information, I knew,
was supposed to assure me that everything would be fine. But
my mind went in another direction entirely. All I could think was
that we had *already* defied the odds by having a child with Down
syndrome. Who was to say we wouldn't flout the odds again?

*Those who dwell continually upon*

*their expectations are apt to become oblivious*

*to the requirements of their actual situation.*

CHARLES SANDERS PIERCE

The trauma of a major disappointment or painful loss tends to break down your defenses. You find it hard to expect much of anything for fear of being disappointed all over again. We went ahead with the shots…but not without anxiety.

On the heels of a painful loss, relief can come as we revise our expectations to better fit the reality of our current situation. Remember—what is, is. To continue to hang on to expectations that are unsupported by the facts will simply intensify our struggle. If we want to improve the quality of our lives while grieving our losses, we have to learn to let go.

On several occasions since Nathan's traumatic entry into this world, I have had to take inventory of my expectations and make some adjustments.

*I can't expect* Nathan to read a book out loud, as Jessie and Ben did when they were in kindergarten. If I hang on to that expectation, I will be disappointed. But *I can expect* him to read. That is a tangible, reachable goal for him.

*I can't expect* that John and I will be empty nesters in six to twelve years, as we had previously thought. But *I can expect* that whatever comes will in some way be good and that God will be with us.

*I can't expect* myself to do as much for John, Jessie, and Ben as I did before Nathan joined our family. Their needs have changed, and so have mine. I'm dividing my energies among four rather than three. But *I can expect* God's strength to be sufficient for every situation. And because His plan is perfect, the whole is greater than the sum of the parts. Nathan has added more to the family than he has taken away. We have all made adjustments, and the experience we share is rich. Different from what we expected, yes, but rich.

*I can't expect* myself to always be a wise, patient, and attentive mother and wife. I want to be, of course, but many times I fall short. When I'm tired, I snap at my kids. When they give me flak, I raise my voice. Although I try very hard, I'm not always who or what I want to be.

What I *can expect* is that God will pour grace over my weaknesses, as I offer them to Him, and restore my strength.

In times of weakness I realize once again how profound and desperate is my need for God and His power to change me. That's when I have to hold tightly to the expectation that He will finish the work He has started in me. That's when I must stand on the promise that His power in me "is able to [carry out His purpose and] do superabundantly, far over *and* above all that we [dare] ask or think [infinitely beyond our highest prayers, desires, thoughts, hopes, or dreams]" (Ephesians 3:20, AMP).

Life doesn't always dish out what we expect. But if we remain open to new possibilities, the road ahead can be an adventure. The scenery may not be what we would have chosen, but it can be very, very good indeed. One way or another, God will get us to our final destination in heaven. And then, He promises, *every expectation we've ever had will fall absurdly short of reality.*[3]

---

*As a man gets wiser he expects less,*

*and probably gets more than he expects.*

JOSEPH FARRELL

---

# CHAPTER NINE

# REFOCUS

WHEN WE ARE IN THE PROCESS OF LETTING GO OF disappointment or a painful loss, we need to check our focus. Ask yourself:

- Am I focusing on my losses, or on my gains?
- Am I staring at a closed door behind me, or getting ready to walk through a new door in front of me?
- Am I clinging to an ending, or preparing for a new beginning?
- Am I complaining about things I can't change, or am I changing the things I can?

When Nathan was born, cards and letters poured in from family and friends. They wanted so much to help and share our grief. One letter enclosed a newspaper clipping that challenged me to open my heart to the new direction my life had taken. It helped me see that by focusing on what I didn't have, instead of on what I did, I was causing much of my own anguish.

The clipping was a little story penned years ago by Emily Perl Kingley. Anticipating the birth of a baby, she wrote, is like planning a fabulous vacation. Then delivery day comes, the wheels of the jumbo jet touch down, and you awaken from your slumber to hear a flight attendant's cheery voice say, "Welcome to Holland."

*"Holland!"* you exclaim. "What do you mean, *Holland?* I signed up for Italy! I'm supposed to be in Italy. All my life I've dreamed of going to Italy."

But there's been a change in the flight plan. They've landed in Holland and there you must stay.

The important thing is that they haven't taken you to a horrible, disgusting, filthy place, full of pestilence, famine, and disease. It's just a *different* place.

So you must go out and buy new guidebooks. And you must learn a whole new language. And you will meet a whole new group of people you would never have met.

It's just a different place. It's slower paced than Italy, less flashy than Italy. But after you've been there a while and you catch your breath, you look around, and you begin to notice that Holland has windmills. Holland has tulips. Holland even has Rembrandts.

But everyone you know is busy coming

and going from Italy, and they're all bragging about what a wonderful time they had there. And for the rest of your life, you will say, "Yes, that's where I was supposed to go. That's what I had planned."

And the pain of that will never, ever, ever go away, because the loss of that dream is a very significant loss. But if you spend your life mourning the fact that you didn't get to Italy, you may never be free to enjoy the special and very lovely things about Holland.[1]

Shifting our focus from what we don't have to what we do have brings a quiet calm to a heart torn with conflict. Peace comes when we make a simple choice to take a deep breath and say to ourselves, *I am exactly where I am supposed to be at this moment.* It means that we stop wasting precious time and emotional energy wishing things were different, longing to be someone else, or wanting another set of circumstances. Refocusing can lead us away from despair toward a greater sense of well-being as we trust that "my times are in Your hand" (Psalm 31:15, NKJV).

---

*As we begin to focus upon God, the things of the Spirit will take shape before our inner eyes.*

A. W. TOZER

---

It doesn't matter what the circumstance is. It may be singleness or widowhood. It may be a heartbreaking marriage, infertility, disability, betrayal, a child gone astray, job loss, or a lingering illness. Whatever the life situation is in which we find ourselves with no control, we can *refocus*. With Paul we can learn to concentrate on "whatever is true, whatever is noble, whatever is right, whatever is pure, whatever is lovely, whatever is admirable...anything [that] is excellent or praiseworthy" (Philippians 4:8).

This mental discipline is part of the "secret" that Paul described a few verses later:

> I know what it is to be in need, and I know what it is to have plenty. I have learned the secret of being content in any and every situation.... I can do everything through him who gives me strength.
>
> PHILIPPIANS 4:12-13

As life would have it, there will be many times when you and I will find ourselves in a "different place." That much is clear. But *God* will be with us in that different place. And as we open our hearts to Him, He will give us the strength we need to carry on. He will carry us through our disappointments and painful losses to a place of acceptance and peace.

That doesn't mean we won't feel sad now and then. We will.

That doesn't mean we won't play the "What if?" game. We will.

That doesn't mean we will never daydream about "Italy." We will.

But as time passes, we will do so less and less.

I am grateful that God has taught our family to perceive Nathan's differences as unique qualities to be appreciated and understood. I am grateful that the joy over what Nathan can do far surpasses the sadness over what he cannot do. As time has passed, a shift in focus has enabled us to clearly see that there's a lot of love in Holland.[2]

---

*The first thing that Jesus promises is suffering:*
*"I tell you...you will be weeping and wailing...*
*and you will be sorrowful."*
*But He calls these pains birth pains.*
*And so, what seems a hindrance becomes a way;*
*what seems an obstacle becomes a door;*
*and what seems a misfit becomes a cornerstone.*
*Jesus changes our history from a random*
*series of sad incidents and accidents into a*
*constant opportunity for a change of heart.*

HENRI J. M. NOUWEN

---

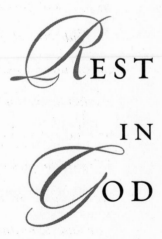

## CHAPTER TEN

REST

IN

GOD

ONE OF THE MOST DIFFICULT-TO-HANDLE ASPECTS OF letting go is time. Healing usually doesn't come all at once and often doesn't come as fast as we would like. When suffering lingers, we have moments when we wonder if we have what it takes to endure. We're not sure we can persevere through the pain. We glance behind us and see the looming disappointments. After a severe loss, our psychological defenses are down, and we tend to forecast more gloom and doom. But morosely obsessing over the past or frantically fretting over the future does nothing to help us heal.

There's another way—a way that leads to rest. Centuries ago, the prophet Isaiah wrote: "[God] will keep in perfect peace all those who trust in him, whose thoughts turn often to the Lord!" (Isaiah 26:3, TLB). Rest comes as we live in the moment— not in the past or the future—with an awareness that God loves us and wants to heal our anguish. As we let go of whatever we're squeezing in our relentless grip and simply trust Him, the empty spaces in our souls become the places God fills with the healing power of His presence.

*In grief nothing "stays put."*
*One keeps emerging from a phase,*
*but it always recurs. Round and round.*
*Everything repeats. Am I going in circles,*
*or dare I hope I am on a spiral?*

C. S. LEWIS

Children have a knack for living in the present and trusting those who love them. They are less concerned about the cares of life, the worries of tomorrow, and the regrets or mistakes of the past. They simply give their full attention to the moment, to whatever they are doing, and enjoy it to the fullest.

It's amazing what kids can teach us about life. I want to close this book with a story that I have reflected on many times while facing the harsh realities of this world. It's a snapshot from a time in my life when I was deeply mourning the losses my little boy suffers because of Down syndrome. The Lord sometimes speaks to me in pictures. This was one of those occasions. One afternoon as I watched Nathan in physical therapy, God taught me a lesson about letting go and resting in Him.

Shortly after Nathan was born, we enrolled him in an early intervention program in which therapists exercised his mind and body to enhance his development. As an infant, Nathan's interventions were one-on-one; but as a toddler, he was moved into a classroom setting with several special-needs children.

During the first part of class, the children met in a large, open room where a physical therapist led them in exercises designed to strengthen muscle tone and develop motor skills. Upbeat music filled the room while the children made their best efforts to accomplish simple toe touches, arm reaches, handclaps, bends, and stretches.

I recalled watching similar routines when Jessie and Ben were in preschool. "Head and shoulder, knees and toes," the kids had chimed along with the tape, keeping their motions in cadence with the music. Their movements jibed with the beat. Their actions were precise, clearly defined, and consistent. But Nathan's class was a much different picture. The children's motions were awkward and rarely in sync with the leader's. If one of the children happened to dance in rhythm, it was more often than not a happy accident.

But a day came when Nathan lit up with a sense of pride while delivering a perfect performance. He was in step with the therapist through the entire song. He didn't miss a beat. All his gestures were right on the mark. It wasn't because John and I had practiced with him umpteen times at home, and it wasn't because his muscle tone had miraculously changed from floppy to firm.

On that particular day, Nathan had been selected for a demonstration. The therapist asked him to come to the front of the room and stand facing the class while she stood behind him.

"Nathan, lean back into me and put your hands in my hands," she instructed.

I watched Nathan relax his body into hers and place his little hands in her palms. When the music began, the therapist guided Nathan's arms through the routine. *One, two, three, four. Up, down, all around. Together. Apart. Clap, clap, clap.*

Nathan's droopy little arms did everything they were supposed to do as he let go and yielded to her lead. His assignment was to lean in and relax. The rest of the work was up to the therapist. Nathan's weakness was his greatest strength that day.

I embarrassed myself during that class. There we were in the middle of "up, down, clap, clap, clap," and I was wiping tears from my eyes. I secretly wondered if the other parents were thinking, *What's the big deal? She sure gets worked up over her son being picked to lead exercises!*

But it had nothing to do with what was going on inside me. The Lord was talking to me through my son. He showed me my need to lean back and rest in the safety of my Father's arms. He nudged me to let go of the things that were troubling me.

With a keen awareness of my own handicaps, I sensed the Lord reassuring me that His grace is sufficient for me. Should I lose my balance and stumble over bumps on my journey, God will steady me and hold me up. When I get out of step, He will help get me back in sync. The greater my weakness, the greater God's strength.[1]

I don't have to be strong to be strong. Nor do you. And we can ease our pain by resting in the Lord…

…by living in the here and now,

…by leaning into God's sovereignty,

…by letting go and letting God take care of the rest.

As we learn to rest in God, time becomes our friend. As it passes, we begin to experience spiritual and emotional healing.

One day we realize that we don't feel quite as much pain today as we did last week or last month. We laugh a little more, and the black cloud that comes and goes isn't quite as dark and doesn't hang around as long. We remember, but the pain diminishes. We begin to realize that the days of mourning are giving way to newfound joys.

114

---

*How shall we rest in God?*

*By giving ourselves wholly to Him.*

*If you give yourself by halves, you cannot find full rest;*

*there will ever be a lurking disquiet*

*in that half that is withheld.*

*Martyrs, confessors, and saints*

*have tasted this rest, and*

*"counted themselves happy in that they endured."*

*A countless host of God's faithful*

*servants have drunk deeply of it under*

*the daily burden of a weary life—dull,*

*commonplace, painful, or desolate.*

*All that God has been to them*

*He is ready to be to you.*

JEAN NICOLAS GROU

---

We have considered a number of strategies that can help us let go of life's disappointments and painful losses. As we learn to let go of them, we will grow beyond and be transformed by them, and disappointment and pain will no longer be the defining qualities of our lives. In God's economy our losses become our gains. Disadvantages become advantages. When we entrust our *disappointments* into God's hands, they become His *appointments* for divine intervention. He does not allow the waves of grief washing over us to destroy us. Instead He uses them to redirect our lives.

Because of our belief in a home beyond this world, we can be realistic about the deaths that come our way, without becoming hopeless. We don't have to get stuck in perpetual sorrow or bitterness. Grief has its proper place, but it is temporary—an episode in our journey, not the whole story.

The cycle is continual. It is progressive. Rarely do we pass through it just once while we are letting go of something important to us. It's kind of like peeling an onion. After we peel one layer, we become aware of something underneath that needs attention. With new awareness come fresh emotion and the need to face, embrace, and process the pain—and then let it go. In time we sense that new depth of character, emotional maturity, and spiritual awakening are coming to the surface. As we come to the end of ourselves, we enter into a vital new intimacy with God.

Jesus said:

"Are you tired? Worn out? Burned out on religion? Come to me. Get away with me and you'll recover your life. I'll show you how to take a real rest. Walk with me and work with me— watch how I do it. Learn the unforced rhythms of grace. I won't lay anything heavy or ill-fitting on you. Keep company with me and you'll learn to live freely and lightly."

MATTHEW 11:28–29, *THE MESSAGE*

We look on the woes of the world.
We hear the whole creation, to use Paul's language, groaning
and laboring in pain.
We see a few good men vainly striving
to help the world into life and light;
and in our sense of the awful magnitude of the
problem and of our inability to do much, we cry out:
"Where's God? How can He bear this?
Why doesn't He do something?"
And there is but one answer that satisfies: and that is the
Incarnation and the Cross.
God could not bear it. He has done something.
He has done the utmost
compatible with moral wisdom.
He has entered into the fellowship
of our suffering and misery and at infinite
cost has taken the world upon His heart.

BORDEN P. BROWNE

"This is how much God loved the world:
He gave his Son, his one and only Son.
And this is why: so that no one need be destroyed;
by believing in him, anyone can have
a whole and lasting life."

JOHN 3:16, *THE MESSAGE*

# GROUP

## DISCUSSION

## QUESTIONS

### CHAPTER 1: RELAX AND RECEIVE

1. What are you finding difficult to let go of at this time in your life?

2. When we grasp and cling, we become emotionally constricted, lose the ability to move forward in our lives, and feel stuck. Can you recall a time in your life when you experienced these things? Please explain.

3. Read John 12:23–25, 27–28 again. What was Christ's perspective on letting go? What is His promise to you?

4. Why is letting go such hard work?

5. What do you hope to receive from God as you learn to relax your grip? Along with the rest of your group, commit these hopes to God in prayer.

### CHAPTER 2: RECOGNIZE THAT WHAT IS, IS

1. Letting go is a process, not an instantaneous event. Can you recall times in your life when you've had to go through it? Describe your thoughts and feelings during that time.

2. What happens when we deny, block, stuff, or numb the pain surrounding our disappointments?

3. When you suffer emotional pain, how do you typically respond? Do you tend to keep the feelings inside, or do you tend to let the feelings out?

4. What did Sarah's story teach you about coping with pain?

5. God often displays His divine power through our weaknesses. What weakness would you like to invite God to touch and use for His glory? As a group, please pray for one another in these areas.

## CHAPTER 3: RELINQUISH CONTROL TO GOD

1. Read John 15:1–2. Can you recall a time in your life when God's pruning changed you for the better? Please explain.

2. Surrender often opens the door to the grieving process. Have you experienced this in your life? How?

3. Do you sense God wanting you to relinquish areas of control? What are they?

4. When we let go, we stop trying to do the impossible and focus on what is possible. How can you apply this idea to your life this week?

5. Why do you think relinquishing control to God is so difficult? Pray for one another to grow in the ability to surrender to God.

## CHAPTER 4: REMEMBER

1. Read Psalm 77 again. What do you learn about David from his expression of emotion in this psalm?

2. Can you recall pivotal experiences of God's loving activity in your life? Please share some of those incidents with others in your group.

3. What makes it difficult for you to remember the times God has been good to you in the past?

4. In the text I asked the question: Doesn't it make sense to build your faith on what you *do know* instead of on what you *don't know?* Make a list of what you *do know,* and share it with your group.

5. Join together in prayer and offer thanks for the times God has been good to you in the past.

## CHAPTER 5: RUN TO GOD

1. When you are deeply disappointed, what is your first natural reaction?

2. Where do you typically "run to"?

3. Read John 9:1–3. What was Jesus trying to teach His disciples?

4. Jeremiah 29:11–13 is God's promise to you. What does this mean with regard to the disappointments you suffer?

5. Can you recall a disappointing situation in your past where it was obvious that God was with you, helping you, and working things out for your good?

6. Set your mental channel this week to look for what God can do in the midst of your difficulties. Commit this goal to God in prayer, asking for the Holy Spirit to fine-tune your spiritual perception. Get together with your group again next year and tell them what you saw.

## CHAPTER 6: RELEASE THE FEELINGS

1. What do you think about the concept: *feeling as healing?*
2. Letting go requires us to feel and ride out our painful emotions. What painful emotions are you enduring at this time in your life?
3. How can people support you in this process? What will you do to let them know?
4. Are you more of a "fighter" or a "flighter"? Please explain.
5. What part of Karen's story was most meaningful to you and why? Pray individually for all the people in your group to grow in their ability to constructively release their feelings.

## CHAPTER 7: REVISIT THE BASICS

1. Do you tend to look out for everyone else's needs at the expense of your own? If so, why do you think that's the case?
2. Why is it so important to take good care of ourselves when we're in the process of letting go of something near and dear to us?
3. What is one small step you could take this week to improve your eating habits? Your sleep? Your exercise?
4. Jesus said, "Love your neighbor as yourself." What are some practical ways to love yourself?
5. Sometimes the pain of letting go can be so consuming that we simply need to shift down into survival mode. What does "survival mode" mean to you? Pray together, asking God to show you some concrete, specific ways you can improve your self-care. Ask Him to empower each group member to follow through with these ideas this week.

## CHAPTER 8: REVISE EXPECTATIONS

1. Read Job 30:26 again. Can you recall a time when you said something similar? Tell the group about it.

2. Suppressing emotion is like trying to hold a beach ball under water. No matter what you do, it will keep popping up. I gave an example from my life. How have you seen this happen in yours?

3. Read Luke 9:23–24. What does this say to you about your expectations?

4. Do you need to revise your expectations to better fit the reality of a current situation? Please explain.

5. What can make it difficult for you to revise your expectations? What can make it easier? Pray as a group, asking God to give you wisdom and insight as you revise your expectations.

## CHAPTER 9: REFOCUS

1. Check your focus. Are you clinging to an ending, or preparing for a new beginning? Share your thoughts about this with your group.

2. What did the "Welcome to Holland" story convey to you?

3. Read Psalm 31:15. Describe your reaction to this comment: "I am exactly where I am supposed to be at this moment in time."

4. Are you in a different place than you expected to be? Explain.

5. God changes our history from a random series of sad incidents and accidents into a constant opportunity for a change of heart. How have you changed as a result of your painful losses? Offer prayers of thanks for the good and very special things about your life as it is today.

## CHAPTER 10: REST IN GOD

1. When we let go, our disappointments and pain do not become the defining qualities of our lives. What does?

2. One of the most difficult ingredients of letting go is time. Have you ever had moments when you wondered if you had what you needed to endure? Talk about it with your group.

123

3. What did my story about Nathan in physical therapy say to you?

4. Read Matthew 11:28–29. What do you hear the Lord saying to you through these verses?

5. Resting in God brings renewal, refreshment, and peace. Join in a time of prayer for one another, asking God to help each person rest in Him in order to more effectively let go of disappointments and painful losses.

Multnomah Publishers
The publisher and author would love to hear your comments about this book. *Please contact us at:*
www.multnomah.net/lettinggo

# NOTES

## CHAPTER ONE

1. Billy Graham, Billy Graham: *The Inspirational Writings* (Dallas: Word, 1995).

2. Dr. Pamela Reeve, *Parables of the Forest* (Sisters, Ore.: Multnomah, 1989).

## CHAPTER TWO

1. Pam Vredevelt, *Angel Behind the Rocking Chair* (Sisters, Ore.: Multnomah, 1997), 103–4.

2. Ibid., 104–5.

3. Ibid., 15–20.

## CHAPTER THREE

1. Pam Vredevelt, *Angel Behind the Rocking Chair* (Sisters, Ore.: Multnomah, 1997), 23–6.

2. Ibid., 31–3.

3. Ibid., 26–8.

4. Ibid., 33–4.

## CHAPTER FOUR

1. Questions adapted from Alan D. Wright, *The God Moment Principle* (Sisters, Ore.: Multnomah, 1999), 14.

2. These words were frequently spoken by my great-aunt Mildred Williamson.

## CHAPTER FIVE

1. Pam Vredevelt, *Angel Behind the Rocking Chair* (Sisters, Ore.: Multnomah, 1997), 161–3.

## CHAPTER SIX

1. Jean Lush and Pam Vredevelt, *Women and Stress* (Grand Rapids: Baker Books, 1992), 17.
2. Pam Vredevelt, *Angel Behind the Rocking Chair* (Sisters, Ore.: Multnomah, 1997), 158–9.
3. Pam Vredevelt, *Espresso for a Woman's Spirit* (Sisters, Ore.: Multnomah, 2000), 161–73.

## CHAPTER EIGHT

1. Pam Vredevelt, *Angel Behind the Rocking Chair* (Sisters, Ore.: Multnomah, 1997), 115.
2. Pam Vredevelt, *Espresso for a Woman's Spirit* (Sisters, Ore.: Multnomah, 2000), 193–4.
3. Ibid., 116–7.

## CHAPTER NINE

1. Emily Perl Kingley, from an October 1992 "Dear Abby" column appearing in the *Oregonian*.
2. Pam Vredevelt, *Angel Behind the Rocking Chair* (Sisters, Ore.: Multnomah, 1997), 112–4.

## CHAPTER TEN

1. Pam Vredevelt, *Espresso for Your Spirit: Hope and Humor for Pooped Out Parents* (Sisters, Ore.: Multnomah, 1999), 124–6.

# You *Can* Worry Less

Letting Go

OF
WORRY
AND
ANXIETY

PAM VREDEVELT

Attention, chronic worriers: It is possible to reduce the intensity, frequency, and duration of painful episodes of anxiety without medication. Licensed counselor Pam Vredevelt draws from twenty years of clinical experience, scientific research, and scriptural insight to offer the reader tools for living a more peaceful and tranquil life. While worrying is for many a deeply embedded habit, because it was learned, it can be "unlearned." With compassion and sound advice, Pam shows how.

ISBN 1-57673-955-4

# A Fresh Java Jolt for the Weary

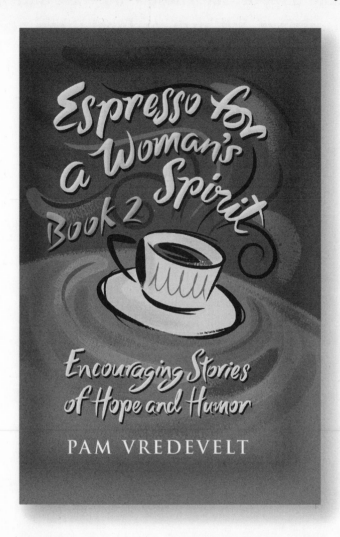

No one has limitless resources. Sooner or later, all of us will find our cup of enthusiasm draining or even downright dry. But just as espresso jump-starts a sluggish mind, *Espresso for a Woman's Spirit, Book 2* will reenergize the lagging spirit! Pam Vredevelt's funny and poignant real-life stories remind readers that God is always faithful, always at work, and always full of everything we need, including guidance, love, compassion, and strength. Each "sip" of this heart-warming book provides just the right amount of get-up-and-go for those whose vigor has "gotten up and gone."

**ISBN 1-57673-986-4**

# Hope and Support for Those Who Have Suffered a Miscarriage, Stillbirth, or Tubal Pregnancy

PAM VREDEVELDT

EMPTY ✻
ARMS

Hope and Support For Those Who

Have Suffered a Miscarriage, Stillbirth

*or* Tubal Pregnancy

Having lost a child, the author writes with compassionate insight to women and their families, addressing grief, anger, guilt, spiritual battles, and other pertinent topics.

ISBN 1-57673-851-5